HIGH SCHOOL FOOTBALL
IN TEXAS

HIGH SCHOOL FOOTBALL
IN TEXAS

AMAZING FOOTBALL STORIES
FROM THE GREATEST PLAYERS OF TEXAS

JEFF FISHER

Sports Publishing books may be purchased in bulk at special discounts for sales promotion, corporate gifts, fund-raising, or educational purposes. Special editions can also be created to specifications. For details, contact the Special Sales Department, Talos Press, 307 West 36th Street, 11th Floor, New York, NY 10018 or info@skyhorsepublishing.com.

Sports Publishing ® is an imprint of Skyhorse Publishing, Inc.®, a Delaware corporation.

Visit our website at www.sportspublishing.com.

10 9 8 7 6 5 4 3 2 1

Library of Congress Cataloging-in-Publication Data is available on file.

Cover design by Tom Lau
Cover photo courtesy of the *Katy Times*

Print ISBN: 978-1-68358-181-9
Ebook ISBN 978-1-68358-182-6

Printed in the United States of America

To Trish

Your love and support have taught me that all things are possible from the moment I became your fellow TV anchor on the 10 o'clock news. Living, working, and playing together is easy when you meet "the one."
Forever and Always!

Table of Contents

Introduction: It Starts with a Simple Question   *xi*

Chapter 1: Raymond Berry—Paris High School—
Paris, Texas   1

Chapter 2: Bill Bradley—Palestine High School—
Palestine, Texas   8

Chapter 3: Drew Brees—Westlake High School—
Westlake, Texas   18

Chapter 4: Earl Campbell—John Tyler High School—
Tyler, Texas   30

Chapter 5: Andy Dalton—Katy High School—
Katy, Texas   38

Chapter 6: Eric Dickerson—Sealy High School—
Sealy, Texas   47

Chapter 7: Derwin Gray—Judson High School—
Converse, Texas   55

Chapter 8: "Mean Joe" Greene—Dunbar High School—
Temple, Texas   65

Chapter 9: Ken Houston—Dunbar High School—
Lufkin, Texas   72

Chapter 10: Craig James—Stratford High School—
Houston, Texas   78

Chapter 11: Bob Lilly—Throckmorton High School—
Throckmorton, Texas   86

Chapter 12: Andrew Luck—Stratford High School—
Houston, Texas   93

Chapter 13: Don Maynard—Colorado City High School—
Colorado City, Texas   99

Chapter 14: Mike Singletary—Worthing High School—
Houston, Texas   105

Chapter 15: Lovie Smith—Big Sandy High School—
Big Sandy, Texas   110

Chapter 16: LaDainian Tomlinson—University High School—
Waco, Texas   117

Chapter 17: Elmo Wright—Sweeny High School—
Sweeny, Texas   125

Chapter 18: Texas Heisman Trophy Winners   133

    Tim Brown—Woodrow Wilson High School—
        Dallas, Texas   134

    Baker Mayfield—Lake Travis High School—
        Austin, Texas   138

    Johnny Manziel—Tivy High School—
        Kerriville, Texas   143

    Robert Griffin III—Copperas Cove High School—
        Cooperas Cove, Texas   146

    The Others   149

Chapter 19: Offensive Players   152

    The Quarterbacks   153

    Sammy Baugh—Sweetwater High School—
        Sweetwater, Texas   153

    Chase Daniel—Southlake Carroll High School—
        Southlake, Texas   155

    Y. A. Tittle—Marshall High School—
        Marshall, Texas   158

The Running Backs   162

    David Overstreet—Big Sandy High School—
    Big Sandy, Texas   162

    Adrian Peterson—Palestine High School—
    Palestine, Texas   164

The Receivers   167

    Dez Bryant—Lufkin High School—
    Lufkin, Texas   167

    Johnny "Lam" Jones—Lampasas High School—
    Lampasas, Texas   170

The Linemen   173

    Forrest Gregg—Sulphur Springs High School—
    Sulphur Springs, Texas   173

    Jerry Sisemore— Plainview High School—
    Plainview, Texas   175

Chapter 20: Defensive Players   179

Defensive Linemen   180

    Brad Shearer—Westlake High School—
    Austin, Texas   180

    Gene Stallings—Paris High School—
    Paris, Texas   182

Linebackers   185

    Jessie Armstead—Carter High School—
    Dallas, Texas   185

    Von Miller – DeSoto High School—
    DeSoto, Texas   187

    Tommy Nobis—Thomas Jefferson High School—
    San Antonio, Texas   188

Defensive Backs   190

Darrell Green—Jones High School—
    Houston, Texas 190
Charles Tillman–Copperas Cove High School—
    Copperas Cove, Texas 192
Chapter 21: Lone Star State Legends 194
    Ken Dabbs—Freer High School—
    Freer, Texas 195
    Todd Dodge—Thomas Jefferson High School—
    Port Arthur, Texas 198
    Johnathan Gray—Aledo High School—
    Aledo, Texas 204
    Kenneth Hall—Sugar Land High School—
    Sugar Land, Texas 206
    Alan Lowry—Irving High School—
    Irving, Texas 214
Chapter 22: Prairie View Interscholastic League 218
    Cliff Branch—Worthing High School—
    Houston, Texas 220
    Jerry LeVias—Hebert High School—
    Beaumont, Texas 221
    Bubba Smith—Charlton-Pollard High School—
    Beaumont, Texas 224
    Charley Taylor—Dalworth High School—
    Grand Prairie, Texas 225
Chapter 23: The Top Texas High School Football Teams
Sending Players to the NFL 227
    Ball High School Tornadoes NFL Alumni 228
    South Oak Cliff High School Golden Bears
    NFL Alumni 229
    NFL Players All-Time by State 231
    NFL Players All-Time by Schools 231

Introduction: It Starts with a Simple Question

DURING MY 40-PLUS years as a sports journalist, I learned one very important lesson when it comes to interviewing professional football players who are generally guarded about what they'll say in front of a microphone. That lesson is, if I know a little bit about the player's hometown and high school football team, I can have a conversation that loosens them up to the point where I can get a couple of interesting answers that become quotes for my story.

A smile usually spreads across a player's face if I ask a question about their high school football team that includes their school's nickname. Almost all of the time that question leads to a great conversation about high school football and beyond. Most players are impressed that I've taken the time to learn a little bit about where their careers began.

I tell this story because it's the heart of this book as I interview some of greatest players from the high school football–crazed state of Texas. I take them back to their roots to tell stories about their favorite high school football games and memories.

In 1990, author Buzz Bissinger wrote a book that would ignite a high school football franchise that now includes a movie and television show. Little did he know the title of the book would establish Friday Night Lights as *the* phrase when it comes to the game of high school football in America. Friday Night Lights is the perfect way to describe what happens every Friday in the fall for some 14,000 high school football teams across America.

Every year, across America, approximately 1.1 million players take to the gridiron with hopes of making it to the "next level." If one is good *and* lucky enough, a player may graduate from Friday night to playing college football on Saturdays. Then comes the ultimate—playing on Sundays as a professional football player in the National Football League.

While high school football is played in every state, plus the District of Columbia, Texas is the center of the universe for the sport. During the 2016 season, according to the National Federation of State High School Association's (NFHS) annual participation survey, 1,069 schools played 11-man football in the Lone Star State, with 163,922 athletes taking to the gridiron. To put that number in perspective, California had 1,017 schools playing the game in 2016 but with just 97,079 participants.

For smaller rural areas, Texas also offers six-man football with 139 schools and 3,329 participants playing a scaled-down version of the game on an 80-yard field, instead of the standard 100-yard playing surface.

Based on the numbers, the odds are stacked against players making it to the NFL. According to statistics from the NFHS, during the 2016–17 school year, 73,063 or 6.9 percent of high school seniors advanced to play college football at the Division I, II, and III levels. If a player was lucky enough to be part of the 73,063, the odds of making it to the pros dropped dramatically. In 2016–17, only 1.6 percent of college football seniors made it to the NFL.

Bottom line: the NFL is made up of kids that had enough talent, heart, and luck to beat the odds.

For those lucky enough to play in the NFL, the last rung on the ladder is to be immortalized in bronze in the Pro Football Hall of Fame, located in Canton, Ohio. As of 2017, 310 players have been enshrined in Canton. Twenty-five of those honorees hail from the Lone Star State, which ranks third nationally. (California leads the way with thirty-seven.)

Texas' Hall of Famers create a *Who's Who* list in the sport with names like Raymond Berry, Earl Campbell, Eric Dickerson, "Mean Joe" Greene, Bob Lilly, and LaDainian Tomlinson to name a few. There's also a good crop of current players like Drew Brees, Von Miller, and Adrian Peterson, who will likely grace the halls of Canton one day. But, for every Hall of Famer, there are hundreds of NFL players who stay well connected to their high school glory days.

And while there has been a slight drop in the number of high school football players across America, the sport in Texas continues to grow with over a billion dollars being spent to improve and develop the sport.

One example of the Texas high school football boom is that school districts across the state have started to build multimillion dollar stadiums to showcase the next generation of Texas high school football players.

For example, Allen High School in the Dallas-Fort Worth metroplex made national news in 2012 with the opening of Eagle Stadium, which seats 18,000 fans and cost $60 million to build. Not to be outdone, the high school football-crazed town of Katy, west of Houston, built a $70 million stadium for the start of the 2017 season. The state's championship games at the Dallas Cowboy's AT&T Stadium have been known to draw over 50,000 fans.

Bottom line, the numbers don't lie: high school football in Texas is a BIG deal. Even George H. W. Bush mentioned high school football during his speech when accepting the Republican nomination for president at the Republican National Convention on August 18, 1988, in the Louisiana Superdome in New Orleans.

Underneath the numbers are hundreds of thousands of stories that Texas high school football fans love to tell and retell about their homegrown players who have gone on to play Sundays on the big stage. Because the of gigantic media microscope that NFLers play under, fans generally know the professional side of Texas' native sons. In this book, I will be taking fans inside high school memories of past and current players as told to me firsthand.

I believe you'll enjoy reading what Drew Brees *didn't* do during his first freshman scrimmage at Austin's Westlake High School. You'll find out why HOF cornerback Ken Houston didn't start playing football until he was a sophomore at Dunbar High School in Lufkin—and then why he did. You'll learn fun facts, like what the legendary SMU Pony Express of Eric Dickerson and Craig James did in their final year of high school football. And what position did "Mean Joe" Greene *really* want to play?

You'll find it all out and more while learning (if you don't know already) why football is so beloved in the heart of Texas.

1

Raymond Berry—Paris High School— Paris, Texas

WOULD YOU BELIEVE that Raymond Berry didn't start a game until his senior year at Paris High School? Not only is it the truth, but Berry (who played for his father, Mark Raymond Berry) didn't even catch a lot of passes during his high school days.

Yes, the Hall of Fame wide receiver for the Baltimore Colts, who played 13 seasons in the NFL and retired in 1967 as the NFL's all-time leader in receptions (631) and receiving yards

(9,275), remembers that high school receptions were few and far between.

"Back then I was a left end in a single-wing formation," recalled Berry, who was inducted into the Pro Football Hall of Fame in 1973. "We had just a few pass plays, not much at all. We basically ran the ball all the time and only threw it once in a while."

Berry added, "Thinking back, I probably caught a couple passes a game, so maybe I had 20 catches for the season. We really just pounded the ball on the ground."

Raymond Emmett Berry Jr. was born on February 27, 1933, in Corpus Christi, Texas, where his father Mark Raymond Berry was the head football coach at Corpus Christi High School from 1931 through 1937. In 1938, Berry's father moved his family to Paris, Texas, to become the head coach of the Paris Wildcats, a program that he led for twenty-five years.

The younger Berry, who was five when his family moved to Paris, said that as he looks back on his childhood in Paris, it really was an ideal town to grow up in.

"The simplicity of Paris was great," said Berry. "The town was heavily agricultural at that time, surrounded by farms that grew cotton. The population of the town was made up of people that were down to earth. I really learned a lot as a kid that is still with me today.

"There's no place I would have rather grown up but in Paris," Berry continued. "I still think it is one of the best towns in the United States of America, and I'm happy to call it my hometown."

As far as playing for his dad, Berry said that there were no special favors, and his small stature didn't help.

"I was very slow growing physically," said Berry. "I only weighed about 135 pounds during my junior year. I played a little bit here and there that year and finally started my senior season. If I recall, I think I was the only end we had on offense, but that wasn't unusual because we were such a small town and only so many players were available.

"Dad treated me like he did everyone else. I don't think he really saw personalities. He was bent on putting a team out there that knew how to play the game and keeping it simple."

As far as growing up, Berry said he might have weighed 150 pounds by the time he graduated Paris High.

Some of Berry's favorite memories of his father were when he talked about meeting legendary Notre Dame University head coach Knute Rockne during a coaching school in South Bend, Indiana.

"Dad went to see Rockne for two years in a row," recalled Berry. "I remember him coming home and saying to me, 'Son, he was the best public speaker I ever heard,' and my father was always talking about his time with him."

The 1949 season was a good one for the Wildcats, who opened with a 20–7 win over Sulphur Springs. While this game didn't stand out on the surface, looking back, it featured two future Hall of Famers in Berry and Forrest Gregg of Sulphur Springs. My research couldn't find a newspaper report on the game, other than the final score with Gregg listed as being a member of the 1949 Sulphur Springs High School football team.

After the Sulphur Springs win, Paris improved to 3–0 with a 7–0 shutout of Kilgore and a 13–6 win over Longview. The fourth game of the season featured two undefeated teams as the

Wildcats took to the road to play Corsicana. Paris fell behind 21–0 before getting on the scoreboard, but the Wildcats couldn't mount a comeback in the 28–7 loss. Newspaper reports from the game indicate that Paris completed eight passes, but there's no mention of how many Berry may have caught.

Paris rebounded the following week with a 13–7 win over Palestine. The Wildcats' defense then kicked things into high gear with back-to-back shutouts against Bonham and Denison.

"Our defense was very good that year," Berry said. "It was definitely the strongest part of our team."

A 39–14 defeat of Sherman gave the Wildcats a 7–1 record heading into the game that Berry called his most memorable. The November 11 match-up with Gainesville for the District 7-AA championship.

"Gainesville is a town that's about a hundred miles from Paris," said Berry. "It was a huge game because the year before, Gainesville made it to the state playoffs, and if we beat them, we would win the district and qualify for the postseason.

"I remember that dad had me calling the plays on offense. We only had about eight or nine plays in the single-wing. With that few, we knew how to run them," joked Berry.

Paris captured the district title with a 13–7 victory, but Berry said the game was in doubt until the end.

"Gainesville was inside the 10-yard line, somewhere near the goal line, and we held them at the very end," said Berry, who played both offense and defense. "Back then, defense was what I was known for. In today's football, I'd be an outside linebacker, but then I was a defense end playing out of a three-point stance. I really enjoyed playing with my dad and my teammates."

Paris closed-out the regular season by shutting out Greenville, 20–0, which gave the Wildcats a 9–1 regular season. The win over Gainesville moved Paris into the Class 2A state playoffs where it faced powerful Highland Park from the Metroplex. During the mid-'40s, Highland Park featured two future Pro Football Hall of Famers in Bobby Layne and Doak Walker. While Berry said there wasn't a whole lot to talk about in the Wildcats' 33–0 loss to Highland Park, he does remember the scene before the start of the game that was played in Paris.

"Being from the Dallas area, they had a large squad," said Berry. "It seemed like when they stepped off the train it was an endless stream of players. They had great depth on that team, and that hurt us since we had a small squad that went both ways."

Berry's senior season was good enough to land him honorable mention on the *Dallas News'* All-State Team that was released at the end of the season.

• • •

One of the unique things about Paris is that the town has two major football figures. Aside from Berry, College Football Hall of Fame coach Gene Stallings hails from the town. Stallings was a freshman when Berry was a senior at the school.

Berry and Stallings had the distinction of facing off against each other as NFL head coaches in the 1986 AFC-NFC Hall of Fame Game that was played in conjunction with that year's Pro Football Hall of Fame induction ceremonies in Canton. The game served as the kickoff to the NFL exhibition season. It remains the only time that two men from the same high school have matched wits against each other as head coaches in an NFL game, even if it only was an exhibition.

Berry was coming off a great year, leading the New England Patriots to their first-ever Super Bowl, where the Pats lost to the Chicago Bears 46–10 in Super Bowl XX. That earned Berry Coach of the Year honors. Stallings was entering his first year as the head coach of the St. Louis Cardinals.

Berry and Stallings both enjoyed the highly unusual match-up—as did the town. A local travel agency even put-up a billboard promoting travel to the game in Canton. The agency called it "The Great Paris Showdown."

"A big group of people from Paris decided they would get together and go to that game and at halftime make a presentation to Raymond and me," recalled Stallings, who estimated about 100 to 150 people from Paris traveled to Canton. "They started talking to the people at the Hall of Fame about what they wanted to do, and the Hall of Fame officials said, 'You've got it all wrong, this is the Pro Football Hall of Fame, and at the halftime we recognize all of the pros that are going into the Hall of Fame.'"

Stallings said that residents of Paris tried to sway the Hall of Fame officials by saying, "'You don't understand, Coach Berry and Coach Stallings are both from Paris.' That's when the Hall of Fame people said, 'No, *you* don't understand, this is the Pro Football Hall of Fame Game.' So what we did was while the pros where being driven around the field in convertibles at halftime, we went down into the end zone and the people of Paris gave us each a plaque. I still have mine."

"Quite honestly, I don't think at the time that Gene or I were aware of the true significance of the moment. If I can remember

correctly, the two of us may have talked about the farming industry around Paris at the time," chuckled Berry.

"I've always been a great fan of Raymond," said Stallings. "He's
represented Paris very well. He's had a great career, and I'm very
fond of Raymond."

AFTER HIGH SCHOOL

With really only one full year as a high school starter, Berry
played Junior College football at Schreiner Institute, which is
now Schreiner University in Kerrville, Texas. He then transferred
to Southern Methodist University where in three years he caught
only 33 passes. Berry also played outside linebacker and defensive
end despite weighing only 180 pounds.

Berry was drafted in the 20th round of the 1954 NFL Draft
by the Baltimore Colts. After playing his entire career with the
Colts, Berry retired in 1967.

2

Bill Bradley—Palestine High School— Palestine, Texas

FOR THOSE WHO are wondering if this Bill Bradley is the same person who made a name for himself as an Olympic basketball player from Princeton University, who went on to a Hall of Fame NBA career with the New York Knicks before entering into politics, becoming a United States Senator…the answer is no. *This* Bill Bradley is a Texas high school football legend and high school All-American that won a state championship in come-from-behind fashion before becoming a star for the Texas

Longhorns that led him to becoming an NFL All-Pro free safety with the Philadelphia Eagles. And way before Bo Jackson and Deion Sanders made playing in the NFL and Major League Baseball a thing; Bradley may have been good enough to do that sort of double duty in the early '70s.

William Calvin Bradley was born on January 24, 1947, in Palestine, Texas. Bradley's exploits on the football field for Palestine High School led to the nickname "Super Bill," but that's getting a little ahead of the story.

Palestine, pronounced *PAL-e-steen*, is a town of about 18,000 in the Piney Woods of East Texas. Aside from Bradley, the small town has produced two other NFL players—running back Adrian Peterson and linebacker Guy Brown, the latter of which played with the Dallas Cowboys in the late '70s and early '80s.

Bradley's father, who worked on the railroad, was a baseball coach. As a young boy, Bill dreamed of playing professional baseball. How good was Bill? Good enough to be selected as a shortstop in the seventh round of the 1965 Major League Baseball Amateur Draft by the Detroit Tigers. Bradley said that he may have become a major leaguer if it wasn't for the fact that when he went to the Tigers' minor league team in Montgomery, Alabama, he became homesick and returned to Texas to take a football scholarship at the University of Texas under legendary head coach Darrell Royal.

"There's no doubt about it, my first love was baseball," said Bradley. "My dad was a baseball coach for twenty-seven years. I grew up playing games of pepper with him all the time. I can honestly say that I played catch with my dad *every* day of my life as a kid."

Bradley was a true multisport athlete who began his football career when he was in seventh grade. Aside from baseball and football, Bradley played basketball and competed in track and field. Because of injuries on the basketball team, Bradley actually was called up to the varsity squad as a freshman, but his varsity football career didn't begin until he was a sophomore.

"I competed with two other guys, I believe, and won the starting quarterback job at the start of my sophomore year," recalled Bradley. "We ran the I-Sprint-out system, which allowed me to throw the ball running. I could run pretty fast back then. I ran the 100-yard dash in 9.8 seconds."

One unique thing about Bradley's athletic talent, and added to the "Super Bill" legend, is the fact that he's ambidextrous. He throws with his right hand, writes with his left, and punts with his left leg. He was a switch-hitter in baseball.

Bradley said because he was so involved with all sports in high school that he really doesn't recall many games or moments during his sophomore and junior seasons in football. However, his memory becomes much more focused when it comes to his senior season in 1964. It's the season when "Super Bill" arrived to become an East Texas high school football hero.

The season began with Palestine ranked as one of the top teams in the state in Class AAA. The team, under the direction of head coach Luke Thornton, featured eight returning starters from a 1963 team that finished 8–3.

"Coach [Luke] Thornton was a great guy and was a bit of an innovator," said Bradley. "For example, back in the '60s, coaches didn't want you drinking water during practice. Coach Thornton made it mandatory to take water breaks. In fact, Coach actually made, with the help of people in the shop class, a device that allowed five or six players at a time to drink water. At that time, it was a big deal.

"Another thing he did was change up the numbers players wore," Bradley added. "For example, our center wore No. 42, our guard had No. 35, and our tight end was No. 78, and what that would do is confuse the defense—especially when we ran an unbalanced line. The defense never knew who the receivers were. It was pretty sly of Coach. And because of what coach did with the numbers, the next year, the University Interscholastic League made it mandatory that centers wore a number in the 50s, guards were in the 60s, tackles had to have a number in the 70s...all because of Coach Thornton."

Every preseason media report suggested that the Wildcats would make a state championship run with most outlets suggesting that a berth in the title game was a forgone conclusion. One reason was because of Bradley who was not only the team's top player but rather one of the top players in the state. Before Palestine played its first game, the Wildcats moved to the No. 1 team in the state rankings in Class AAA. That raised the team's confidence going into the season opener against Athens.

As high as the Wildcats' confidence was going into the Athens game on September 11, 1964, it was that low coming out of the game after Athens upset them, 27–8.

The Athens game woke up Palestine, which began to roll behind a defense that was shutting down opponents right and left. Coming into the October 30 game against Kilgore, the Wildcats' defense hadn't allowed an opponent to score more than a touchdown in any of the games after their initial loss.

"Our district [District 7-AAA] was good," Bradley said. "Every game was nip-and-tuck with not a lot of points being scored. I remember a lot of games in the district were 7–0, 8–7, and 14–7. A lot of guys in our district went on to play Division I football, so the competition was always good."

Palestine and Kilgore brought 3–0 district records into the showdown on Kilgore's home field. It was this game when the legend of Super Bill began, although if you search newspaper archives you'll find a different story about the quarterback that could throw touchdowns passes with both hands.

The myth about the right-handed/left-handed quarterback is that he threw a game-winning touchdown pass with his left hand in an incredible come-from-behind victory in the state semifinals. The truth about Super Bill throwing a touchdown with his left hand occurred in the game against Kilgore that Palestine won, 28–16.

"So the real story is…yes, I'm ambidextrous. I can throw left handed, but not as good as with my right," said Bradley. "So in the Kilgore game, a guy hits me just as I release the ball and my hand got caught up against my shoulder pad on the chest plate. The guy's helmet just hit my hand, and it fractured a bone in the top of my hand. I still have a knot there to this day.

"So on the next play, we're down at the 7-yard line or so and I roll-out to the left on a sprint out," Bradley continued. "I see our receiver is wide open, so I decided to throw the ball with my left hand for a touchdown. If you could get film of that pass, you'd see that it actually looked like a helicopter…it was not a spiral. He was so wide open that all my receiver had to do was *not* drop the ball."

Bradley chuckled throughout telling that story but said the truth is the pass wasn't really a helicopter, but people like to hear it because it adds to the myth.

What is fact, not fiction, is that Palestine brought a nine-game win streak into the Class AAA playoffs. The Wildcats opened the postseason with back-to-back shutouts. In the opening round Bi-District game, Palestine gained revenge against Athens with an 8–0 victory on the Hornets' home turf.

The rematch was played on a muddy field in inclement weather. Each team was bogged-down offensively with Palestine only gaining 152 yards of total offense. The Wildcat defense limited Athens to 58 yards of total offense, with neither team completing a pass. In fact, Bradley only attempted one throw, which equaled the one pass attempt by the Hornets.

The game's only score was set up by a 32-yard punt return in the second quarter. After returning the ball to the Athens' 3-yard line, Bradley tried a quarterback sneak that gained one yard to the 2-yard line. On the next play, Ronnie Jones scored the game's only touchdown. Bradley's two-point conversion pass to Bob Stephenson completed the scoring.

In the state quarterfinals, the Palestine defense continued to play well in a 22–0 shutout of Bonham, which never got deeper than the Wildcat 33-yard line. With the defense pitching its second straight shutout, Bradley had the offense humming. He was a perfect 4-for-4 in the passing department with three touchdown passes.

One of the interesting things that Palestine did all year long was have the mentality that they were never playing an away game.

How'd they do that? They would take dirt and grass from their home field and sprinkle it wherever they played.

"We never played on a foreign field," Bradley said. "We had a ceremony before every away game we played, and we sprinkled the dirt and grass everywhere we went. Another thing we did was someone made a sign that we put above our locker room door that read, 'Through these doors pass the toughest team in District 7 AAA.' Any time you went in or out of the door, you had to touch it."

Palestine was riding an 11-game win streak coming into the AAA state semifinals against Wichita Falls' Hirschi High School, which upset undefeated Andrews in the state quarterfinals. To this day, this game is considered one of the all-time best in the Lone Star State.

Hirschi High jumped-out to a 23–0 lead before 9,000 fans in Arlington. The Huskies maintained that lead until about two minutes were left in the third quarter.

"Simply put, we were getting killed," recalled Bradley.

With about 14 minutes left in the game, Bradley's running and throwing talents took over to write the next chapter in the legend of Super Bill.

Bradley capped a 63-yard scoring drive with a 4-yard touchdown run that cut the deficit to 23–6. He then completed the two-point conversion try with a pass to Bob Stephenson to make it 23–8 heading into the fourth quarter.

After holding Hirschi on its next possession, Bradley and his teammates went to work on an 80-yard drive that only took four plays and ended with Bradley tossing a 29-yard TD pass to John

McDonald. Another two-point pass completion between Bradley and Stephenson cut the lead to 23–16 early in the fourth quarter.

"Things just started to come together," recounted Bradley. "My receivers were outstanding, making acrobatic catches in the fourth quarter. Then there was Jerry Reeder ripping off a long touchdown run [65 yards] that got us to within a point."

Palestine attempted its third straight two-point conversion, but it failed, leaving Hirschi with the lead at 23–22.

"I remember the end of the game very well," Bradley said. "They [Hirschi] had the ball around our 45 with a fourth and one…and they didn't punt. They wanted to try to ice the game. Our defense stopped them on fourth down, but the reality of it is, if they had punted instead of going for it, we probably wouldn't have had enough time with two minutes left to go the length of the field."

Palestine then took over around its own 45. Battling the clock, Bradley and his teammates went to work on their game-winning drive.

"I take the snap, and all of a sudden, I'm running around scrambling a bit," remembered Bradley. "Finally, the clock is at zero, zero, zero, and I throw it into the end zone and a buddy of mine, Curtis Fitzgerald, goes up and catches it between two players, and we win the game. It was crazy, it was just a throw to hope to Jesus and somehow he [Curtis] went up and came down with it."

Now, back to the myth. Some 50-plus years later, some claim that that touchdown was the one that Bradley threw with his left hand.

"No, it was the Kilgore game that that happened," chuckled Bradley. "I get a lot of credit for that game, but we had a great team on both sides of the ball. You have to remember, about a dozen guys on that team went on to play major college football."

Bradley ended the game completing 10-of-17 passes for 201 yards and two touchdowns, including the game winner. That moved the Wildcats into the state championship game against San Marcos at Texas A&M's Kyle Field in College Station. The Rattlers were the only team in Texas at that point with an undefeated record.

It was a cold December day when Palestine met San Marcos and, once again, Bradley was the catalyst on defense first and then on offense. Early in the first quarter, Bradley picked off a Rattlers' pass and returned it to the San Marcos' 11-yard line. Two plays later Super Bill threw a touchdown pass that started a 24–15 victory, giving Palestine its first and only state football championship.

"To be honest, the championship was a piece of cake, compared with the state semi," Bradley said. "Those games created a lot of great memories that I still enjoy to this day."

AFTER HIGH SCHOOL

With his dreams of being a Major League Baseball player behind him, Bradley went to Texas where he began his career as a quarterback and punter for the Longhorns. He became a starter during his sophomore season in 1966. He held the starting job into his senior season, but that was when Texas introduced the wishbone formation. After a slow start, Coach Royal moved Bradley to wide receiver and then over to defensive back on defense.

The Philadelphia Eagles drafted Bradley in the third round of the 1969 NFL Draft. He was a three-time Pro Bowler with the Eagles and named First Team All-Pro in 1971 and 1972. Bradley became an assistant coach at the college and professional levels after his eight-year NFL career.

3

Drew Brees—Westlake High School— Westlake, Texas

WHEN DREW BREES'S football career comes to an end, the guy that everyone said was too small to play quarterback in the NFL will be taking up residence in the Pro Football Hall of Fame. There's no doubt that the third player to ever top 70,000 passing yards in his professional career will be inducted into Canton after he hangs up his helmet.

However, there was plenty of doubt at the start of Drew's high school career at Westlake High School in Austin. Brees's Hall of

Fame career got off to an inauspicious start, when he didn't play in his first scrimmage.

"I'll never forget it, he was the only player that didn't play in that scrimmage," recalled Drew's dad Eugene "Chip" Brees, who is a lawyer in Austin. "After the game, I really wanted to go over and talk with the coach, but I didn't want to be a helicopter parent, so I decided against it.

"You have to remember, Drew didn't play tackle football until ninth grade, because he played flag football up until that point," Brees's father continued. "He wasn't part of the Westlake feeder system, so at the start of his freshman season he was fourth or fifth on the depth chart."

"I really didn't know who Drew Brees was when he arrived at Westlake," said Ron Schroeder, the legendary head coach at Westlake, who amassed a record of 187–23–3 during his career. "Drew wasn't in our feeder system, because he was at St. Andrews [Episcopal School], so I didn't know what he could or couldn't do, but I knew he had only ever played flag football."

"At that point, there wasn't anything very special about him, so the coaches put him on the Freshman B Team. There are always a lot of players to get in during that first scrimmage. The coaches shouldn't have let that happen, but it did."

Drew Christopher Brees was born on January 15, 1979, in Austin, Texas, to parents who were athletically talented. Eugene "Chip" Brees played college basketball at Texas A&M, while his mom Mina Akins was also a very good basketball player. She was All-State in basketball, plus she played volleyball and was a cheerleader.

The Akins family was loaded with football talent. Mina's brother Marty Akins was an All-American quarterback at the University of Texas from 1975 through 1977. In fact, he is the only wishbone quarterback to ever be an All-American. In high school, Marty was the Texas High School Football 3A Football Player of the Year in 1971, when he led Gregory-Portland High School to the state championship game. As a junior high and high school quarterback, Marty owned a record of 60–4–1.

Drew's grandfather, Ray Akins, is a Texas High School Football Hall of Fame coach who won 302 games over thirty-eight years. Akins was the coach at Gregory-Portland High from 1965 through 1988. When he retired, he was the second winningest coach in Texas high school football history.

When Drew was a child, he and his younger brother Reid spent a lot of time with their grandfather on his farm.

"Drew would spend time each summer with Ray," recalled Drew's dad Chip. "Drew and his brother Reid would work with Ray on his farm, and I know that he put them through the paces. As much as they may have griped about how hard he made them work, I know they both benefited from it."

"He loved being out there, working on fences, feeding the cows, checking on the heifers, doing all that stuff…and that's what I got to do with him," said Drew Brees. "Lots of good times."

Near the end of the 2017 NFL season, Drew's grandfather passed away at ninety-two years of age.

"He was probably one of the most incredible people, incredible men that you could ever meet," said Brees after his grandfather passed away in late in December 2017. "They just do not make them like that anymore, honestly. He was ninety-two years old.

He lived an incredible life. He taught me so much about life, about respecting others, caring for others, about discipline, and about hard work.

"Obviously, he was a football coach for thirty-eight years so there was plenty of ball being coached along the way, but more so than that—just spending time with him. Watching him and my grandmother, they modeled us for what a relationship and marriage should look like. They were married for sixty-seven years, and that is pretty remarkable. A guy who grew up from very humble means in Brady, Texas, which if you look at a map of Texas is in the dead center of Texas."

"Drew evidently gets his competitive nature from his grand-daddy," said Ken Dabbs, who was an assistant coach and recruiting coordinator at the University of Texas, who recruited Earl Campbell and over a dozen All-Americans to the Austin Campus. "Ray, his grandfather, and I went way back, because I grew-up in Freer, Texas, and helped him get his job at Freer High School where he won five district championships. He was a great coach."

Ironically, Dabbs is also the person that started the high school football program at Westlake High School in Austin, when he was hired as the school's first head coach in 1969. Dabbs said that while he's never met Drew, he and his grandfather had plenty of chats about him during his junior and senior seasons.

Heading into his sophomore year, Brees was the quarterback on the Junior Varsity B team. The quarterback of the JV A team was Jonny Rodgers.

"Jonny was the guy that we were grooming for varsity," recalled Schroeder. "I remember we had a scrimmage and Jonny hurt his knee. Our JV coach said that Drew was the JV B Team quarterback, so we decided to move him up. Truthfully, if Jonny hadn't gotten hurt, I don't know if Drew would ever have gotten a chance."

For historical perspective, Jonny was the younger brother of Jay Rodgers, who played quarterback at Indiana University from 1996 through 1998. The boys' dad is Randy Rodgers, who was then in charge of recruiting at the University of Texas when John Mackovic was the Longhorns' head coach.

"That year with Drew as the JV quarterback, it was the best JV team we ever had," said Schroeder. "And that was really the first time that I started recognizing him as a football player because of the impact he had on the JV team."

Schroeder remembered that in Brees's first start with the JV A Team, he completed all but one pass for over 300 yards and four touchdowns. The JV team went a perfect 10–0.

Schroeder said that while Drew's sophomore season was a good one, it didn't give him the inside track to the varsity starting job the following year. Schroeder, who also served as Brees's quarterback coach, said he worked a lot with him and all of the quarterbacks during the offseason.

"Drew doesn't like this story that I tell about him, but its true and it shows how far he has come," Schroeder said. "I had this drill on the dip bar that strengthens the triceps muscles, which is important when it comes to throwing the football. What they would do is jump up on the bar and then lower their chest to the elbows and then jump back up. Well, when Drew went to do it, he couldn't do one. So what I let him do was jump up to extend his arms and then let him sink down and then jump up.

"He really wasn't that impressive at that age as an athlete. He ran a 4.9 second to 5 flat 40, and he really wasn't that impressive in the weight room, but he was just a really good kid and you liked being around him. He was ready to be a quarterback mentally but maybe not physically. He was very savvy when it came to his football aptitude."

"There were a lot of high expectations going into Drew's junior year because of the great senior leadership on that team," said Chip. "Drew was actually the question mark heading into the season, because he hadn't started on the varsity level yet. Once he got his sea legs under him, the team started rocking and rolling."

"You know as a coach that you're always going to get a bunch of personalities on a team and you're never sure if they're all going to mesh," Schroeder said. "But when it comes to Drew, there's something about his personality that makes people mesh around him."

Westlake got off to a great start in 1995 with a team that featured three guys that would make the second team of the Class 5A Texas All-State squad at the end of the season. Protecting Brees up front were All-State players Rod Beavan and Seth McKinney. Running back Ryan Nunez also made second team All-State, with Brees earning honorable mention on the squad.

With Brees at the offensive controls, Westlake finished the regular season a perfect 10–0. The Chaparral offense scored over 50 points in three games and scored a season-high 63 points against Austin High School.

After close playoff wins over San Antonio Madison and San Antonio Marshall, which ended in a 15–15 tie that the Chaps won on penetrations, it looked like Westlake had a shot to win a state championship, but Brees's junior season came to a halt in the third round of the Class 5A Division II playoffs against Alice High School.

On the third series of the game for Westlake, Brees rolled-out to pass when he was hit by Alice's Benny Godines, who was listed as being about 5-feet-6-inches tall. Brees hobbled off the field, never to return due to a knee injury, which turned out to be a torn anterior cruciate ligament.

● ● ●

Westlake would go on to beat Alice, 42–20. But with Jonny Rodgers filling in for Brees, the Chaps lost to San Antonio Roosevelt 28–14 in the state quarterfinals. Roosevelt went on to win the state championship that year. The Chaps finished with a 12–1–1 record, with the tie coming against Marshall that they won on penetrations.

While the torn ACL was a sad ending to Brees's junior season, his final year of high school may have been a preview of what was ahead for him.

"Drew spent the spring and early summer rehabilitating his knee," said Chip Brees. "I think he only went to the Stanford camp that year, because he was still in his brace and maybe at about half speed. Looking back on the knee injury, he was better for it, because he had to work through a problem."

Schroeder added, "He really didn't do anything full speed until August, which is one of the reasons he lost out on recruiting opportunities."

Westlake didn't enter 1996 with a lot of hype since they only returned two starters on offense—Brees and offensive lineman Seth McKinney, who was second team All-State in 1995.

McKinney would go on to play at Texas A&M and then nine years in the NFL with three different teams. McKinney's contributions in 1995 were diminished on the day of Westlake's first game when he broke his foot during the school's pep rally. He did return sometime around the middle of the season, but the weight of the offense at the start of the year was on Brees.

"Yes, we didn't return a lot on offense, but Drew had a really good team around him," said Schroeder. "But the key to Drew is he makes the people around him better than they really are because they enjoy playing with him. He did a great job that year of getting the team camaraderie going."

The regular season was perfect for Westlake with the offense scoring less than 30 points only one time, which was in the season opener against San Antonio Holmes. Heading into the postseason, the Chaps were averaging 41.9 points per game.

The postseason began with a 20–10 win over San Antonio MacArthur, followed by a 33–19 win over San Antonio Clark in the second round. The third round saw the Chaps shutout Victoria Memorial 41–0, and that's when the offense really started to heat-up for the stretch run to a state title.

Drew's dad recalls that at the start of the Victoria game, the team got a little extra emotion when the Victoria cheerleaders unraveled a sign for its team to run through that read "something along the lines of 'Westlake, you can't buy this game.'"

"Westlake had a reputation of being a wealthy district," said Chip Brees. "I remember after the game Drew said that the team saw that sign while they were standing on the sidelines and it really got them fired up."

"At that point in the season, we were playing really well, and everyone was playing hard," recalled Schroeder. "I remember the game against San Antonio Churchill [state quarterfinals] in the Alamodome. We had a really good game and the kids were rallying. It's a cool time of the year because football is no longer drudgery.

"In that game, Jonny Rodgers was in the middle of the huddle chanting, 'Drew Brees, Drew Brees, Drew Brees,' and the whole team started chanting his name. And then I could see Drew rally around that. Let's face it, you're not going to chant for a guy you don't like."

Westlake beat Churchill 49–21 and never looked back. The Chaps beat Aldine 42–21 in the state semifinals in the Houston Astrodome, which put them into the state championship game against Abilene Cooper, which brought a 12–3 record into the game at Texas Stadium, home of the Dallas Cowboys.

Brees closed out his high school career on a high note whipping Abilene Cooper 55–15. However, the final score doesn't indicate how close the game was with the Cougars taking a 7–0 lead early in the second quarter. The game was tied at the half at 7–7.

In the second half, it was the Drew Brees show as he struck with three short touchdown runs and two touchdown passes. He finished 11-of-18 for 163 yards. All-State wide receiver Ryan Read, who also battled back from a 1995 knee injury, caught three passes, giving him 108 for the season, which set a new Texas state record.

The victory meant that Brees had never lost a high school football game that he started. His record was 28–0–1, which was a big part of Westlake's success in the 90s that saw the Chaps' record stand at 94–8–3 from 1990 through the 1996 season.

For his outstanding senior season, Brees was named the Class 5A Offensive Player of the Year. He finished the season completing 211 of 333 passes for 3,528 yards with 33 touchdowns. For his career, he completed 314 of 490 passes (64.1 percent) for 5,461 yards with 50 touchdowns.

"What impressed me about that season was how his arm developed that year," said Schroeder. "I remember that we started dropping him a little deeper and had our receivers make their break point at 20 instead of 12 yards and then go on a skinny post. And he really could throw that route well, and I remember thinking to myself in practice that wow, he was developing a rifle arm. I really think that that sort of thing caught some of the teams in the early playoff games off guard."

"You gotta remember that Drew was a late bloomer as I mentioned before; that when we first got him he couldn't do a bar dip. That was something fun to watch during his senior season, the way he physically matured."

"That entire senior season was a highlight for me," said Chip Brees. "It would be hard to pick any one particular game, but it was really enjoyable because it was a real family oriented thing. The parents all knew each other. The students rallied around the boys. And what's interesting is that, as a player, as you go to each level, college and the pros, that feeling that we had with Drew at Westlake sort of diminishes a bit. Don't get me wrong, we knew families at Purdue, but that state championship season was special because of the closeness of everyone in the community.

And for the kids just playing for the joy of the game, it was great because most don't go on to the next level."

Brees closed out his high school career being the starting QB for the South All-Stars in the 1997 Texas High School Coaches Association's North-South All-Star game that was played before nearly 15,000 fans in Fort Worth. Drew was 8-of-10 for 143 yards with one touchdown pass. He also scored two touchdowns on short runs. Playing on that same team was LaDainian Tomlinson from University High School in Waco, who became Drew's teammate on the San Diego Chargers and retired from the NFL after the 2011 season while Brees is still performing at a very high level in the NFL.

In 2011, Brees was inducted into the Texas High School Football Hall of Fame, making him the third generation in his family to be saluted for his contributions to high school football in the Lone Star State. His grandfather Ray was inducted in 1992, while Drew's uncle and Ray's son Marty entered the Texas High School Football Hall of Fame five years earlier in 1987.

"I was at those ceremonies," said Brees when he learned about his election into the Texas High School Football Hall of Fame. "I always hoped and dreamed that someday I'd have a chance to be inducted."

AFTER HIGH SCHOOL

Despite being undefeated as a starting high school quarterback, Brees wasn't besieged with college scholarship offers.

"I went and watched a lot of Westlake games in 1996, because I had retired from Texas the year before," said Ken Dabbs, who had started the Westlake program in the late '60s. "I watched Drew play, and I watched him play some more, and the one morning I got up I noticed that he didn't have a scholarship and I couldn't figure it out. So I decided to go to UT and have a meeting with John Mackovic, the head coach at that time, who also had a daughter in the band at Westlake. I said, 'Coach, Drew Brees has never lost a game as a high school quarterback, and he was 16–0 this year and won a state championship, and I was wondering why you hadn't offered him?' The answer was that they didn't like his throwing motion."

With no offers from within the state of Texas, Brees headed to Indiana to play for Purdue where he was a three-year starter. The San Diego Chargers drafted Brees with the 32nd overall pick in the 2001 NFL Draft. He closed out the 2009 season by winning Super Bowl XLIV by beating the Indianapolis Colts, 31–17.

4

Earl Campbell—John Tyler High School—Tyler, Texas

HOW GOOD WAS Earl Campbell? In 1989, former Dallas Cowboys head coach Barry Switzer, who tried to recruit Campbell at John Tyler High School when he was the head coach at the University of Oklahoma, wrote in his book *The Bootlegger's Boy* that Campbell was the only player that could have gone from high school straight to the NFL and immediately become a star.

"Yeah, when I heard that Coach Switzer said that…I had to laugh," chuckled Campbell. "He tried real hard to recruit me.

Even though I decided on Texas, Barry and I are still good friends to this day. As far as what Barry said about me, I'll let other people answer whether I could have gone straight to the pros."

Earl Christian Campbell, the sixth of eleven children, was born on March 29, 1955. He started playing flag football in the fifth grade but rather as a kicker than a running back. Earl's father, B. C. Campbell, died when he was eleven years old and his mother Ann Campbell was not fond of the sport. Even after Earl became more and more of a celebrity figure from high school into the pros, his mom still wasn't a fan of the game.

"I think she liked who I was in the sport," said Campbell, "but I don't think she really ever liked the game at all."

Earl's football talents began to be noticed in the sixth grade as a linebacker, with similarities to the great Dick Butkus of the Chicago Bears.

"I wanted to be the first black Dick Butkus," Campbell said. "I had the Dick Butkus walk down. I had the bowed legs like him. I mean, I had everything down. He was my hero."

About the only time that Earl may have stepped onto a high school football field without someone knowing who he was would have been his first-ever varsity game as a sophomore when John Tyler High School took on Longview High. David Barron was a student at John Tyler at the time and attended Campbell's first game.

"In his first game, he wasn't listed in the program, so nobody knew who he was," said Barron, who went on to become a well-known sports journalist in Texas. "Longview's quarterback that year was Jeb Blount who played for Tulsa [college] and the Tampa Bay Bucs in the NFL. You'd see a play from scrimmage and it appeared as though Blount was stumbling at the line of scrimmage as he dropped back to pass and then went down. This happened a couple of times. After a while it became clear that he wasn't stumbling. Basically, the stumbling was being caused by Earl beating the center off the ball, tackling Blount before he could get back to set up. I believe Earl sacked him eight times that night.

"I don't remember Earl's name being announced on the PA system that night," Barron added, "so it wasn't until the next day when looking in the paper saw his name about seven or eight paragraphs into the story. That was the first time we saw the name Earl Campbell."

During his sophomore season in 1971, wearing No. 20, the 6-foot-1, 180-pound Campbell was named as the Sophomore of the Year in District 14-AAAA as a linebacker. However it wasn't a great season for the team, with John Tyler finishing 3–6–1. For the 1972 season, Corky Nelson took over as head coach with Campbell and twelve starters returning from the previous season. Once again, Campbell was outstanding at linebacker, but Nelson and assistant coach Lawrence "Butch" LaCroix wanted Earl running over people, along with tackling them.

"I remember at some point going into my junior year, Coach Nelson and Coach LaCroix came over to me and said, 'Earl, let's talk.' I said, 'About what?'" recounted Campbell. "Basically, they said they didn't have a running back so they wanted to see how I fit in there. I said, 'No, no, I'm a middle linebacker.' I remember I ran the ball two or three times in practice, and I literally threw the ball down. I played like I was fumbling, because that's how badly I didn't want to play running back. Finally Coach LaCroix, who had a big voice, asked if I'd just try hanging on to the ball and they'd discuss keeping me at linebacker. So on the first carry after that I went about 55 yards to the end zone and did my Elmo Wright dance to celebrate. After that I never got to be a linebacker again."

Truth of the matter is that Campbell was an outstanding two-way player during his junior year. He was first team All-District and Defensive Player of the Year at linebacker while averaging 16 unassisted tackles per game. On offense, Campbell was second team All-District at running back while averaging 11.1 yards per carry. Despite Campbell's outstanding play, the Lions didn't make the playoffs, finishing the season with an 8–2 record.

"Once I decided that I wanted to be a running back, I did everything I could to become the best," said Campbell. "I started watching everything I could on the legendary Jim Brown, because that's the closest person that compared to me. There were a lot of great running backs, but Jim Brown is the guy that flicked my Bic."

Campbell added modestly, "I had a God-given gift. He put me on this Earth to play football, and I made sure that I didn't mess up that gift, so that's what drove me to be the best football player that I could be—especially in high school."

You can't tell the Earl Campbell high school story without bringing in Texas recruiting legend Ken Dabbs. Dabbs, who was one of the first recruiting coordinators in college football, was the man responsible for winning over Earl and his family, which led to Campbell's incredible career at the University of Texas in Austin.

Dabbs, who has an incredible memory at eighty-three years of age, recalls most of his visits to the Campbell's home that could be called sparse at best in 1973. He said he was very nervous to meet Earl and his big family. "The first afternoon I drove up there, I was scared to death. Whenever you go to recruit someone of Earl's magnitude, the very first thing you must do is sell yourself. The next thing you have to do is assess who the decision-maker is. So it didn't take me long to know that Mrs. Campbell was the one that was making the decision. I got Ms. Campbell on my side in a hurry. Really, I recruited her, not him."

What Dabbs did next was brand himself, literally.

"You got to remember, I'm thirty-eight years old, and head coaches like Bill Yeoman of Houston, Grant Teaff from Baylor, and Barry Switzer from Oklahoma had already been there and here I am standing at the front door," chuckled Dabbs. "So now Ms. Campbell and her daughter Evelyn are at the door and Ms. Campbell says, 'Oh no, not another one. How am I going to remember all of you coaches' names?' So I looked at her and said you can remember my name very easily. Think Brylcreem, a little dab will do ya. Just add a 'b' and a 's' on the end and you have my name—Dabbs.

"I stayed there about an hour and then left to go to Shreveport [Louisiana]. On my way back the next day, I thought I'd stop by the house. I go knock on the door, and Evelyn answers it, sees me, and hollers, 'Momma, Coach Brylcreem is here.'"

That 24-hour period led to over a half-century of friendship between Coach Brylcreem and the Campbell family.

"The one thing he [Dabbs] didn't do was shuck and jive," said Campbell about his first couple of meeting with Coach Dabbs. "I remember he had a great sense of humor. Back then when certain coaches would promise you lots of stuff, all Coach Dabbs did was say he could offer me a great education at one of the best universities with the chance to play football."

With only three returners coming back from the 1972 team, nobody expected much out of John Tyler. However, with Campbell playing like a man among boys, the season quickly turned into something special. Earl's twin brothers, Steve and Tim, who both played linebacker, joined him on the 1973 squad.

John Tyler beat Greenville 21–0 on the road to open the season. In the following game, Campbell scored three second-half rushing touchdowns to beat Corsicana, 26–7. He also booted two extra points in the win. After a win over Irving Nimitz, John Tyler High headed into its bye week a perfect 3–0 on the season.

In the fourth game, Campbell did it with his legs *and* his arm. He had touchdown runs for 41 and 19 yards, plus threw a 73-yard touchdown pass in the Lions' 21–16 win over Texarkana.

The wins kept piling up for the Lions, who moved to 5–0 with a 16–0 shutout of Longview with Campbell carrying the ball 24 times for 157 yards (with a 57-yard touchdown run). The next week, the Lion defense put up its second straight shutout in a 33–0 defeat of Marshall. Earl only needed 12 carries to rush for 124 yards and two TDs.

Campbell topped the 1,000-yard rushing mark for the season in the seventh game of the season, when he ran for 147 yards and four touchdowns in a 34–20 defeat of Lufkin. The magical season could have come to an end when Earl suffered a hip pointer in the Lions' 14–7 win over Nacogdoches to improve to 8–0 on the season. Campbell missed the next game, but returned for the regular season finale against Robert E. Lee. The Lions finished a perfect 10–0 with a 28–6 win with Campbell only gaining 81 yards in the game, which is known as the Battle of the Roses for the crosstown rivals.

"I don't remember much about the regular season, but I do recall that we were excited about making the playoffs," said Campbell.

The Lions played in Class 4A, which was the largest classification in the state at that time. They opened up with 36–0 shutout of Plano, which was followed by wins over Conroe (10–7), Fort Worth Arlington Heights (34–12) in the state quarterfinals, and Arlington Sam Houston (22–7) in the state semis. This set up a championship showdown between Tyler and Austin Reagan.

"I remember being told we were playing Austin Reagan for the championship, and I said, 'Where's that?'" Campbell laughed. "I'm from tiny Tyler, and I had no idea where Austin was."

While Earl may not have known where Austin was, Texas high school football fans sure knew about the powerful Austin Reagan program that was going after its fourth state championship in seven years. Many newspapers reported that Campbell and his teammates would be facing their toughest defense to date. Earl entered the championship having rushed for 1,872 yards while scoring 166 points. Earl's twin brothers anchored the Lions' defense that had only given up 79 points in the team's fourteen games.

In the first-ever high school football game played in Houston's Astrodome, Campbell put on a show that cemented him as a high school legend. He ran the ball 32 times for 164 yards and two touchdowns in a 21–14 victory. His 2,036 yards for the year gave Campbell the state record in the Class 4A at the time.

"That was a great feeling," said Campbell about the championship. "I can't really say if there's one great thing from that year, because the whole year was great. I'll let others tell you how good we were because it's not my place to say."

With a state championship in hand, it was time for Campbell to choose his college. With his mother loving the man affectionately known as "Coach Brylcreem," the decision really wasn't that difficult.

"I love that man and his straightforward way," said Campbell. "To be honest, I always thought Coach Dabbs was the head coach until I met Darrell Royal after months of being recruited by Coach Dabbs. I really was shocked that this great man wasn't the head coach of the Texas Longhorns, but I'm happy to say that if it weren't for Coach Dabbs, there would never have been an Earl Campbell at the University of Texas. He's special."

AFTER HIGH SCHOOL

During his four years at Texas, Campbell ran for 4,443 yards, averaging 5.8 yards per carry with 40 touchdowns. Campbell won the Heisman Trophy after his senior season in 1977 and was inducted into the College Football Hall of Fame in 1990.

The Houston Oilers selected Campbell No. 1 overall in the 1978 NFL Draft. He was named the NFL Offensive Rookie of the Year after picking up 1,450 yards with 13 touchdowns. Campbell played with the Oilers and the New Orleans Saints during an eight-year pro career, totaling 9,407 yards with 74 touchdowns. Campbell was elected to the Pro Football Hall of Fame in 1991.

5

Andy Dalton—Katy High School— Katy, Texas

ANDY DALTON MADE the most of his one season as the quarterback of the Katy Tigers. After splitting the quarter-backing duties during his junior year, the current Cincinnati Bengals QB led the Tigers to the state championship in his senior year.

Andrew Gregory Dalton was born on October 29, 1987. His family moved to Katy when he was in first grade. Shortly after becoming residents, Greg and Tina Dalton, who were high school sweethearts, found out in a hurry how important high school football was to the community.

"When we moved to Katy, the kids were four, seven, and nine, with Andy being seven," said Tina Dalton. "We moved into our neighborhood and met one of the neighbors who asked, 'Have you gotten your tickets to the game yet?' I said, 'What are you talking about?' That's when she said, 'The high school football games.' I told her that my kids were so little, so why would I do that right now? She said, 'Well this is what we do on Friday nights. Everybody goes to the games, so you can come with us and you'll see.'

"So that was the start of season tickets to the Katy Tigers high school football games when the kids were really young. It was pretty amazing to just see a sea of red with the whole town coming out. It's just what you did."

"When we first moved out to Katy, we didn't know what a big deal football was there," said Andy Dalton, who grew up playing baseball, basketball, and football in the community. "Everyone is involved, and the community really gets behind the football team, and that's what makes it so cool to play there."

Dalton, who has made the NFL Pro Bowl twice in his career, said there was never a doubt that he wanted to be a part of the Katy Tigers, "When you go to those games and you're really young in elementary school or junior high, you look up to those guys that are on the varsity. It's all you think about. You think this is where I want to get to and this is where I want to be playing.

"I went to Katy Elementary, Katy Junior High, and Katy High, and was a part of it all the way. Once you get to Junior High and you start playing for the school, you're a Katy Tiger. So at that point you're starting to learn the offense you'll be running in high school, which makes you feel a part of it from a very young age as you build your way into it."

"The great thing about playing in high school is you're playing with friends and families that you grew up with," said Greg Dalton, who was a high school quarterback himself in the Houston area at Memorial High School.

There's no doubt that playing with your friends is what makes high school football so cool," Andy added. "When I think back to my time at Katy, it wasn't just our team. The entire town of Katy was behind us and the town really would shut down just like you see in *Friday Night Lights*."

Andy's mom pointed out that he always would go after No. 14, the number his dad wore when he was in high school, and there are some similarities between the two. "They're both very athletic and coordinated," she added. "And I'd say by nature they are both strong leaders."

"We would always throw the ball around in the front yard," said Greg Dalton. "I guess when he was young, I'd try to teach him the way I learned how to throw the ball, but by the time he got to Katy he had a really great quarterback coach."

The main man behind the Katy Tiger success is Gary Joseph, who for over three decades has been part of the Tiger tradition that includes four state championships. After being a longtime assistant at Katy, Joseph became the head coach in 2004. Since then, Katy has appeared in eight state championship games. His overall record is an incredible 190–18 through the 2017 season. Joseph has also led the Tigers to thirteen district titles in fourteen years, and the school hasn't lost a district game since 2008.

"It's a real neat place to coach and work," said Joseph. "We get great support from our administration, the principals, and the athletic directors to make our program be successful. I love it when kids like Andy come back and share stories, because it really is like a family around here."

Like Drew Brees, Dalton's high school career also began on the Freshman B team. Andy didn't make the JV team the following year; instead, he was part of the Katy sophomore team and became a part of the varsity during his junior season.

"I love the game of football, but I never pushed him to play," said Greg Dalton. "When he was on the Freshman B team I remember telling him not to worry about who was ahead of him, because things would work out—and they did. I never really hovered around him. I was certainly interested in what he was doing, but I always let his coaches do the coaching, because he had great coaches at Katy."

"Andy was your typical, normal kid that was making the adjustment from junior high to high school," said coach Gary Joseph. "He had some decent height, but he didn't jump out at you, but he was a kid who knew how to work. As you watched him through the year, you saw the work habits and work ethic develop. By the end of his freshman year, I thought to myself that he had a shot at becoming a decent football player."

"Once you finally make the varsity, that's when you get to put the decal on your helmet. Before that you just have the white helmet," reminisced Dalton. "When you finally get to play what you've been watching your entire life, it's a very cool thing—especially in Katy.

"The one thing I've learned from Coach Joseph is loyalty," continued Dalton. "You have to remember, he was at Katy for so long before becoming the head coach. He was the defensive coordinator and I'm sure he had opportunities to go other places but decided that he wanted to stay at Katy. That loyalty led him to waiting it out, and then when Mike Johnson retired as head coach after my sophomore year Coach Joseph became my head coach."

"The great thing about Katy is we don't have a freshman coach and a sub-varsity coach, all of our coaches are varsity coaches," said Joseph. "What that means is all of the kids get coached by the same guys from ninth through the twelfth grade. By doing that the terminology is all the same. The techniques we're teaching as seniors are the same as we were teaching them as freshmen. That means we're always adding on, instead of constantly beginning at the starting line. It makes all the difference in the world."

Dalton got to watch Katy win a state championship during his sophomore year in 2003, as the third-string backup. During his junior year, he split the quarterbacking duties with Jared Gayhart, who the next spring was taken in the 13th round of the Major League Baseball Amateur Draft as a pitcher.

After a quarterfinal finish in 2004, Dalton got his chance to take control of the offense that he had been working toward for the better part of a decade. It also marked the end of Dalton's baseball career, as he decided to focus solely on football. His parents said that that was one of the hardest decisions he had to make.

"I really enjoyed all sports, but it was a decision that I thought was the best," recalled Dalton.

"At that point the evolution of Andy's maturity was phenomenal," said Joseph. "He took control of the huddle and then he developed physically to the point that he was able to throw an out route to the wide side of the field, which is difficult for any high school quarterback to do. Once we saw that, we knew we had something special."

Dalton and his teammates roared through the regular season without many challenges, finishing a perfect 10–0. Offensively, the Tigers averaged just over 40 points a game during the regular season. After a couple of easy wins in the first two rounds of the Class 5A Division II playoffs, Katy's first challenge of the year was in the state quarterfinals against Cypress Falls.

Cy Falls took a 28–10 lead late in the third quarter, but that's when Dalton went to work. As time ran out in the third quarter, Dalton connected with Michael Fuda on an 80-yard touchdown strike to cut the lead to 28–17. Another Dalton TD pass and two-point conversion got Katy to within three points at 28–25 with 2:10 to play.

Cy Falls was forced to punt after it couldn't move the ball, which led to a blocked punt by Katy. Dalton's 32-yard touchdown pass with 31 seconds to go gave Katy a 32–28 victory to advance the Tigers to the state semis.

"That was one of the coolest games in my memory," said Dalton. "A lot of the fans had left, I think somebody told me that the local newspaper had left because they thought we had lost. At one point in the game, I remember thinking is this going to be it? Is this how my high school football career ends? That game is one that a lot of people still talk about today."

Tina Dalton agreed that it's a game she'll never forget, and Greg Dalton said that it's a game which has stood the test of time. "As fans and a community, I think everyone thought that it was a foregone conclusion that we were going to face Southlake Carroll in the finals. However, here we are in the state quarterfinals against Cy Falls and it looked like we were going to lose. The most amazing thing is that there were Katy fans that were leaving the game early, which doesn't happen. As a dad, the games that I enjoy the most are the most painful games because we got to see, as parents, Andy continue to battle."

In the state semifinals against Smithson Valley, Dalton tossed a touchdown pass in a 17–14 victory that saw the Katy defense need to step-up down the stretch after losing a 17–0 lead.

Coming into the Class 5A Division II championship game, Southlake Carroll was a well-known commodity. Coached by Texas high school football legend Todd Dodge, the Dragons not only were a Texas powerhouse but a national powerhouse after capturing *USA Today*'s "mythical" national high school football championship after a perfect season the year before. The team's fastbreak, spread offense had been putting up points in bunches through the years.

On the other side of the coin, Katy wasn't in awe of the Dragons since the Tigers upset them, 16–15, in the 2003 state championship. That loss was the Dragons' only blemish on their record in the last 63 games. A win by Southlake Carroll would give the school its third state title in the last four years.

"We knew how good they [Southlake Carroll] were," said Dalton.

"We knew from beating them two years prior that we were going to have to be perfect," said Coach Joseph. "We came off two very tough games and knew that there wasn't much room for error against Southlake Carroll. We turned the ball over five times. You can't do that against a great team."

When the curtain fell at Texas Stadium, Southlake Carroll had gone back-to-back with a 34–20 victory, winning its second straight "mythical" national championship. Dalton finished the day with 232 yards passing and two touchdown passes. When all was totaled after the 2005 season, Dalton had an amazing year passing for 2,877 yards with 42 touchdowns. The *Houston Chronicle* named him the Greater Houston Area Offensive Player of the Year.

"That championship game was tough," remembered Dalton. "Things didn't go our way, but they were a really good team. Obviously, we would have loved to have won state, but I don't think it takes away from the year that we had. The expectations at Katy are so high that sometimes people get disappointed when there's not a state title, but as a team and as players it's great to have those memories. And when I get together with my friends that I grew up with, we'll also be able to enjoy that season."

AFTER HIGH SCHOOL

Dalton attended Texas Christian University after Katy. Redshirting his first year at TCU, Dalton became the Horned Frogs' starting quarterback in 2007. As a four-year starter, Dalton amassed a record of 42–7, including a perfect 13–0 record as a senior when

TCU finished No. 2 in the nation in the Associated Press Top 25.

Dalton was selected by the Cincinnati Bengals with the 35th pick in the second round of the 2011 NFL Draft. As a rookie quarterback, Dalton led the Bengals to a 9–7 record and a berth in the NFL playoffs in 2011. He became the first quarterback in NFL history not drafted in the first round to start all 16 games.

6

Eric Dickerson—Sealy High School—Sealy, Texas

EVERYONE REMEMBERS TED Williams's last baseball game, as he topped-off his career with a home run in his final at-bat. Many feel that Sealy High School's Eric Dickerson closed out his high school career with a similar type of feat.

The baseball analogy may not be too far off, as Bill Burttschell, Dickerson's offensive line coach at Sealy, said Eric was very good on the diamond. "Truthfully, from little league on up, Eric was good enough that he probably could have made it to the major leagues. He was a left-handed hitter and a center fielder. He was also very good in basketball as well."

Eric Demetric Dickerson was born on September 2, 1960, in the small town of Sealy, about 50 miles west of Houston. Eric's mom, Helen Johnson, was seventeen at the time of Eric's birth but decided against marrying Eric's dad Richard Seals. Instead of raising him on her own, she decided to allow Eric's great-great aunt, Viola Dickerson, to raise him. He was told that Helen was actually his sister, and eventually Viola adopted him in 1963, which is why Eric's last name is Dickerson. He added that his biological mom lived right next door to him when he was growing up.

Dickerson said growing up was hard because he suffered a lot of teasing when he was young, as he was very skinny and wore glasses. But as far as the family was concerned, he felt only love.

"I didn't grow up rich, but as a family, we managed," said Dickerson, who didn't find out the real identity of his biological mom until he was in his early teens. "We were never hungry. I always had clothes on my back. But we definitely weren't rich."

Dickerson, who was inducted into the Pro Football Hall of Fame in 1999, began playing football in the seventh grade.

"At the start, the coaches played me at free safety and wideout when I was a kid," said Dickerson. "I hated being a wideout. My favorite player was O. J. [Simpson]. They told me I was too tall to play running back, but eventually, I got to playing running back, and I loved it.

"I remember my first game in seventh grade," recalled Dickerson, who wore No. 45 for his first game. "I played on the kickoff and punt return teams. On the opening kickoff, I ran it back for a touchdown. I loved football from that point on."

"Eric was special on the football field, even at the young age," said Burttschell, who grew up in Sealy before becoming a Sealy assistant coach during Eric's junior year.

Dickerson said that his talent on the football field also ended the teasing from the other kids.

Many say that Dickerson's incredible athletic talent may be from his biological father, who he never knew growing up. Richard Seals played running back and defensive back at Prairie View A&M from 1962 to 1965.

Seals, who graduated with a bachelor's degree in physical education and a minor in Spanish, was talented in both football and track where he ran a 4.4 40. He was an All-American running back on the football team that won national championships in 1963 and 1964. Seals is a member of both the Prairie View A&M University Sports Hall of Fame and the Southwestern Athletic Conference Hall of Fame.

Seals was sixteen years old and in tenth grade when Eric was born, and he never really took part in his son's life. In fact, in a 1989 *Sports Illustrated* interview, Dickerson was quoted as saying his father was "dead" when the reporter asked him about their relationship.

Dickerson, who is a very private person, didn't have a great relationship with his high school football head coach Ralph Harris, who coached at the college level at many schools after leaving the high school ranks, including being the tight ends coach at the University of Texas. Harris is described as a disciplinarian.

"As a high school coach, you can have a tremendous impact on a kid, but I didn't like my high school coach, at all," said Dickerson. "We thought he was racist. He was from East Texas and had never coached black players. At one point all of the black players except one quit the team."

That was Dickerson's freshman season, but he returned to the team after talking with an older friend, who suggested that football was Eric's way out of Sealy. While his return to the team didn't mean an end to his issues with Coach Harris, Dickerson did settle into his role as one of the best running backs in the state of Texas.

Dickerson said, "I really thought about transferring to Brookshire Royal High School after the walkout. That's when I talked with my mom who said that I should just go out and play [at Sealy] and that's what I did. And I'm glad I played.

"About a year and a half ago, a black friend of mine was playing golf with him [Coach Harris] and my friend called me. My friend said, 'I've got someone that wants to say hi to you.' As soon as I heard his [Coach Harris] voice, I knew who it was. I could feel my heart beating fast...it was like I was right back in high school. I said how's it going Ralph? I never called him coach, just Ralph. That's when he said, 'I just want to apologize Eric. I want to say I'm sorry. I was an idiot back in those days.'"

Dickerson said the call and apology made him feel good. He said it always amazed him when he and his fellow NFL Hall of Famers would rave about what great relationships they had with their high school football coaches. He said the call from Coach Harris also laid to rest thoughts that he was wrong about his head coach.

"I was just a kid, but I knew I wasn't wrong about what was going on with Ralph," said Dickerson. "When you play sports, it's not about color. That's the beauty of sports…it's about the color of the uniform."

Dickerson, who gained over 6,000 yards rushing during his high school career, said that memories of his sophomore and junior years are vague, but he does have some fond memories of his senior year that ended with a Class 2A state championship.

"Yeah, I really don't think about those days, because they're so long ago," said Dickerson, who also won the state championship in the 100-yard dash with a speedy time of 9.4 seconds. "I do think about my parents and the good times with them. However, I do remember the run to the state championship."

Burttschell said that Eric dominated during his junior year in 1977, but Sealy was in a tough district with Bellville and, back then, teams needed to win the district to advance to the state playoffs. The Brahmas, who were ranked No. 1 in the state, beat Sealy 28–6 during the regular season, which kept the Tigers out of the playoffs. Sealy finished 7–2–1 that year. Bellville advanced to the Class 2A state championship game, where it lost to Wylie 22–14.

The 1978 season was a special one for Eric, his teammates, his coaches, and the town of Sealy. Burttschell said that when it came to the leadership role, Eric led by example. "Eric was the show and was special, but you have to remember we had some other good football players on that team that made it a special team. Prior to that group of kids, Sealy had losing records. However, starting with Eric in junior high school that group of players didn't lose a game before they got to high school."

Before Coach Harris arrived in 1975, Sealy had lost 18 straight. The losing streak hit 22 games before the Tigers got a win under

Harris. The '75 team finished 2–8. During Eric's sophomore season, Sealy was 4–6.

Dickerson entered his senior season listed 6-foot-2, 205 pounds with speed to burn. Heading into the postseason, Sealy was undefeated and ranked No. 6 in the state in Class 2A. The only concern was that Dickerson injured his ankle near the end of the regular season, which caused the coaching staff to use him sparingly during the early round playoff wins against Splendora (31–6) and Hampshire-Fannett (21–7).

Dickerson said he really remembers the team's quarterfinal game that set the tone for the rest of the playoff run. "I remember our quarterfinal game against West [High School] in Austin, and it was cold. The game was close at the half, I believe, and then right after the half I had a 70- or 80-yard touchdown run, and I think at that point, we thought we were going to win state."

Dickerson's memory was pretty much spot on, as the touchdown run was for 73 yards. It was one of three touchdown runs in a 32–7 defeat of West High. He ran for 224 yards, which advanced the Tigers to the state semifinals against San Antonio Randolph High School.

In the state semifinal game at the University of Texas' Memorial Stadium, Dickerson had another outstanding performance with four head coaches from the Southwest Conference—Fred Akers of Texas, Tom Wilson of Texas A&M, Rex Dockery of Texas Tech, and Ron Meyer of SMU—attending the game. Dickerson ran the ball 15 times for 132 yards and four touchdowns. He also caught two screen passes for 71 yards in the 42–18 rout of Randolph.

"Any given night Barry Switzer would be at a game. John Robinson (USC) stopped in the office. Fred Akers would be there a lot. It was a *Who's Who* at any different time during the season," recalled Burtschell.

University of Texas recruiting coordinator Ken Dabbs said Dickerson and Earl Campbell were two very special backs that he had a chance to watch in person. "The biggest difference between the two was that you couldn't tackle Earl. You could tackle Eric *if* you could catch him…boy was he fast."

With his ankle fully healed, Dickerson and his teammates prepared for the state championship game against defending champ Wylie. Sealy were looking to put an end to a perfect season. Eric entered the game at Baylor University in Waco with 2,342 yards and 33 touchdowns.

"One thing I remember about the game is that they [Wylie] wanted us to come closer to them to play the state championship game," recalled Dickerson.

Wylie is located about 20 miles northeast of Dallas. Dickerson said that the team wasn't interested in playing there for racial reasons, since Wylie was a mostly white community. Instead, the two teams decided on Baylor University in Waco for the game.

Without hesitation, Dickerson can rattle off his stats for the title game, "296 yards and three touchdown runs." Those 296 yards set a state championship game record at the time. In addition, Dickerson carried the ball 36 times, scoring his fourth touchdown on a 33-yard pass play in the 42–20 victory.

"The game was close at halftime," Dickerson said. "But the second half was all ours. I remember it well, because my mom was there, Barry Switzer [Oklahoma head coach] was there, Ron Meyer [SMU head coach] was there. It was big."

"My favorite memory was on Eric's final carry in the championship when I think he broke seven tackles on his very last carry and scored," said Burttschell. "He was just a man among boys."

Dickerson finished the season with 2,642 yards and 37 touchdowns, plus was named to *Parade* magazine's All-America team.

"I liked football more in high school and college than in the pros," said Dickerson. "The reason is because back then the NFL really was an ugly business. That state championship was special because it was the first that Sealy had ever won. Yes, there was a lot of segregation in town with blacks on one side and whites on the other, but when we put on that uniform, we were all one color...we were all Tigers."

AFTER HIGH SCHOOL

Dickerson accepted a scholarship to Southern Methodist University, where he teamed up with Craig James, who also won a Texas high school football championship in 1978. Dickerson and James became one of the most famous college football running duos, nicknamed "The Pony Express."

The Los Angeles Rams selected Dickerson with the second overall pick in the 1983 NFL Draft. He rushed for over 13,000 yards in his career and holds the single-season rushing record of 2,105 yards that he set in 1984.

7

Derwin Gray—Judson High School— Converse, Texas

DERWIN "DEWEY" GRAY is a believer in God and football. In many ways during high school, Gray considered football as his God because of a chaotic home life.

"What I mean by football was my god is that football gave me a vision for life that could get me out of my circumstances and get me to college," said Gray, who is the founder and lead Pastor of the Transformation Church in South Carolina, considered one of the fastest-growing churches in America in 2016. "And, it gave me inspiration, because I knew that if you worked hard at football, positive things could happen."

Derwin Gray was born on April 9, 1971, in San Antonio, Texas, where he was raised by his grandmother. As a youngster surrounded by the sheer chaos of violence, drug addiction, and abuse in his family, Gray focused on the big picture while enjoying the game that he always remembers playing.

"I remember when I was a little boy, I always remember playing with the older kids," Gray said. "We would play in the streets and I remember playing quarterback. Then in middle school, when I finally began to play tackle, I remember I was a decent player, but I was a late developer.

"I remember in eighth grade when my middle school football coach told my mom that if I continued to work hard that maybe one day I could get a scholarship. And when my mom told me that, I asked her 'what type of *ship* is that?' Until that point, I had never heard of a scholarship. She then had to explain to me that it's when they pay for you to go to college and you get to play ball. That put a seed in my heart that eventually began to grow."

During his first two years of high school, Gray played at San Antonio's Fox Tech High School. He said he was a decent player as a freshman and sophomore, but when he chose to transfer to Judson High School in the second semester of his sophomore year, he found out everything that he *didn't* know about football.

"I was not prepared when it came to the discipline, the work ethic, and the pace at Judson," Gray said. "The way they worked was light years above me. That's when I entered into what's called 'Rocket Pride,' which is a culture of absolute sacrifice, teamwork, and hard work. We went through this thing called boot camp and

I still don't know how I made it through my first one. Mentally, they pushed you as far as you could go, and then they pushed you physically as far as you could go."

At Judson, Gray played for legendary head coach D. W. Rutledge, who now serves as the executive director of the Texas High School Coaches Association. Rutledge is one of Texas' most successful high school football coaches. He became Judson's head coach in 1984, compiling an overall record of 198–31–5 with four state championships in seventeen years. The football stadium at Judson is named in his honor.

"I remember when he [Dewey] came into our program that he had a lot of athletic ability, but he wasn't in very good shape," recalled Rutledge. "We had a high-tempo practice and he really struggled getting through the practices early on. However, once he got through that, you could tell that he was going to be a really great player.

"He was one of those guys that when he tackled you, he had that striking ability. He had great speed and picked up things very easily. He was a special athlete."

Heading into spring practice for his junior season, Gray remembered that he was either second- or third-string cornerback for the Rockets. He recalled that his position coach was always tough on him.

"Coach [Mike] Sullivan would always make me stay after practice to run sprints to get me into shape," Gray said. "I thought he didn't like me…that he was punishing me. Now, as I look back, I actually realize that he loved me and saw the potential that I had. I wouldn't have made it to the NFL if it wasn't for Coach Sullivan really investing in me and teaching me what hard work was."

"Mike [Sullivan] knew he had to help Dewey get into shape so he would keep him after practice to do a little conditioning with him," said Rutledge. "Mike always pushed the kids pretty hard but, at the same time, he'd take his athletes to the classroom and take them through the SAT and ACT preparation. He and Dewey developed a pretty strong relationship."

"Playing football at Judson was my sanctuary compared to my home life, which was chaotic," Gray said. "Judson offered me structure and discipline. Coach Rutledge never talked about winning games. We talked about leadership, virtues, and character development. Plus, we talked about one day making a difference in the world as a husband and a father."

Gray said he started four games during his junior year, which led to a huge senior season that included playing against the legendary Dallas Carter High School football team that, thanks to Hollywood magic or poetic license, played Odessa Permian in the movie version of *Friday Night Lights* for the state championship. The fact of the matter is that Carter and Permian met in the state semifinals and then Judson played Carter for the state title.

The Gray-Sullivan relationship was tested early in Gray's senior season when he didn't show up for practice and was benched.

"Yeah, I felt entitled and decided that I could miss practice without telling the coaches," Gray remembered. "At Judson, you don't miss practice unless you've been abducted by aliens. So I show up the next day, and I'm second string. We go into that weeks' game, and I'm second string and don't play.

"On Monday, Coach Sullivan and I have this face-to-face, man-to-man talk and I didn't believe that his eyes were capable of crying. All of a sudden he's weeping as we talk and he's telling me that I could be a great player, but I have to earn it. Coach reached out, took my hands and said, 'I have your future in my hands. It's up to you to decide what you're going to do with it.' The next day at practice I was destroying my teammates. I was playing with such urgency and such passion because I realized my hope and my dream of getting out was going to be lost because of me."

However, even with a great week of practice, Gray didn't start the next game either.

"I remember that at some point during that week Dewey came up to me to talk about not playing, and I got after him pretty good," said Rutledge. "And, at one point, I just looked at him and said 'compete.'"

Gray said that is exactly what Coach Rutledge said to him. "I tried to give him the sad puppy dog look, and all Coach said was 'compete.'"

While burning for a chance to play during his second-straight week of not starting, Sullivan finally told Dewy to get into the game on the second defensive play of the game.

"I remember running onto the field and just destroying East Central High School," said Gray. "And I haven't looked back since. Coach Sullivan and Rutledge were masters at bringing out the best in you."

Heading into the playoffs, Judson was 9–1 with the only blemish on their record coming in the second game of the season with a 14–12 loss to San Antonio Clark. Gray said that he has many great memories from his senior season, but one that stands out is the lead-up to the Rockets' second-round playoff game against Alice High School.

"They [Alice] were a lot like us and ran a lot of play action stuff," remembered Gray. "At practice, we were working on one of their expected plays. The first time I didn't cover the receiver because Coach Rutledge was in the way. The second time we practiced the play, Coach Rutledge was in the way again and Coach Sullivan is yelling to do the play again. So we run the play a third time and once again Coach Rutledge is in the way, so I don't cover the guy, because I'm not going to tell Coach Rutledge to get out of the way. Finally, Coach Rutledge said 'Oh, Dewey, I was in the way.' That didn't matter to Coach Sullivan at all.

"So when we get to the game, Alice runs that play three times and I intercept three passes," chuckled Gray. "That taught me one of my greatest life lessons—God doesn't waste anything. Trust his faithfulness and the things that you thought were wasted… God will use for something fruitful and productive."

Judson won that second-round Class 5A playoff game against Alice, 42–0, which would be one of nine shutouts by the Rockets defense in 1988. Four of those shutouts were in the postseason. Aside from the win over Alice, the Rockets shutout San Antonio Jefferson in the first round (47–0), Corpus Christi Carroll in the state quarterfinals (30–0), and Houston Stratford in the state semis (16–0).

With a berth to the state title game in perfect view, the Rocket defense was equal to the task. In the win over Carroll, Judson allowed only 83 yards of total offense and seven first downs. Gray and his defensive teammates were even better in the semis, allowing 61 yards of total offense with five sacks for minus-41 yards.

"They [Stratford] only made it past the 50 once," remembered Gray. "Honestly, we didn't know we were that good, because our coaches never let us rest on our laurels. We were always looking ahead. We were grateful, but with that look ahead mentality we never took our foot off the gas."

"You got to remember we started about six sophomores that year on defense," said Rutledge. "Dewey was the leader of that unit. He wasn't what you would call a rah-rah guy. He could get loud if he needed to do so, but the way he worked hard and practiced is what made him our leader."

The only team standing in the way of Judson winning its first state title since 1983 was Dallas Carter. While the *Friday Night Lights* movie may have been inaccurate in the fact that Carter didn't play Permian for the title, what was factual was that Carter was a big, strong, talented team that was looking to win the first state title for a Dallas Independent School District team since 1950.

Even though the Cowboys were strong on the field, an issue off the field clouded the team's postseason. On an anonymous tip before the playoffs began, the University Interscholastic League began looking into a grade given to Carter's star running back and cornerback Gary Edwards earlier in the semester.

Texas has a "no pass, no play" rule, which means a student isn't eligible to play if he doesn't meet minimum standards in the classroom. A student-athlete must achieve a minimum score of 70 or sit out until receiving a passing score. It was determined that Edwards didn't achieve the minimum standard in his Algebra class, which led the UIL to take Carter out of the playoffs and replace them with South Grand Prairie. However, that wasn't the end of the story. A legal challenge to the UIL's decision ensued, which led to the state's governing body putting Dallas Carter back into the playoffs while the investigation continued into whether Edwards's grade had been manipulated.

"Man, they [Dallas Carter] were so much better than everyone else in the state," said Gray. "Quite honestly though, heading into the game, we thought our defense was every bit as good as theirs."

Eligibility issue aside, Carter roared out to 31–0 lead and never looked back in a 31–14 victory. In the first half, the Cowboys' defense (led by future NFL linebacker Jessie Armstead) held Judson to 60 yards of total offense and just two first downs. For the game, the Carter defense picked off three passes and recovered three fumbles.

"Carter was just loaded," Rutledge said. "We just had a hard time doing anything offensively against that very talented defense."

"They spread us out," recalled Gray, who was named All-State at the end of the season. "Their team speed just demolished us. On defense, they played a [Chicago] Bears' 4-6 defense. They had so many athletes. We had three guys with over a thousand yards rushing, so we didn't really pass the ball at all. They were too fast and physical for us to legitimately run, so we were just overmatched—and we were a phenomenal team."

Within a week of celebrating the championship, Dallas Carter's football community was rocked with news of a robbery ring that involved several members of the championship team. Five days after the title game, three football players robbed a Jack in the Box fast food restaurant with pantyhose pulled over their heads. That was the first of twenty-one robberies that police connected to over a dozen Carter neighborhood teenagers, including six from the football team.

Edwards was sentenced to sixteen years in prison, while All-American defensive back Derric Evans, who had a full scholarship to the University of Tennessee, was also sentenced. But the story didn't end there. In 1990, the UIL stripped Dallas Carter of its state championship, giving the title to Judson.

Looking back, Gray said he's extremely thankful that his coaches cared about him and his teammates like they did. It's something that built a strong connection that he still has to this day to those memories at Judson.

"Love is a verb, love is an action," said Gray. "What they did at Judson is they authentically loved us by building us into men through discipline and hard work and teamwork. Basically, Judson taught all of us about character formation and football was the vehicle to do that."

AFTER HIGH SCHOOL

After graduating from Judson, Gray accepted a scholarship to Brigham Young University in Utah. The Indianapolis Colts selected Gray with the 92nd overall pick in the fourth round of the 1993 NFL Draft. During his time with the Colts, his path to the ministry began when he met teammate Steve Grant, who would walk around the locker room with nothing but a towel and ask his teammates, "Do you know Christ?" Gray said years of talking with the player known as "The Naked Preacher" is what brought him to having his own church.

The story with Coach Sullivan comes full circle in Dewey's fifth year in the NFL. "Coach called me around the same time that I decided to commit my life to Christ. He told me that I needed to come to Texas and we needed to talk. He said he was going through a divorce and his life was falling apart. He was at another school now and there I was in his office, and the roles were reversed, and I led him to Christ in his office."

8

"Mean Joe" Greene—Dunbar High School—Temple, Texas

AT 6-FEET-4 INCHES tall and weighing 275 pounds, nobody would ever mistake "Mean Joe" Greene, the cornerstone of the Pittsburgh Steelers' Iron Curtain defense, as a running back. But that's exactly what the native of Temple, Texas, wanted to be.

"I was a Jim Brown fan. I liked Mr. Spats with Baltimore, Lenny Moore and, of course, Gayle Sayers. Whenever we played a pick-up football game, I wanted to run the football or throw it.

I think I realized during those pick-up games that I wasn't going to be a running back or a quarterback," laughed Greene.

Charles Edward Greene was born on September 24, 1946, during segregation and played at Dunbar High School in Temple. He said he had a fairly normal childhood, but his young athletic talents weren't the things that Hall of Fame careers are made of.

"I was always large, but I never considered myself the macho man," said Greene. "By the time I was in seventh grade, I was tall and probably already weighed about 150 pounds. I remember when it came time for pick-up games, I'd always be the last player picked. I would never tell anyone that I loved the contact of football. To be honest, if anyone tells you that they do, they're not being honest with you."

In addition to what he said was "zero" athletic talent for football, baseball, and basketball, Greene had to worry about being bullied. Yes, the man who would eventually earn the nickname "Mean Joe," was afraid to walk home beginning in the sixth grade. He said that bullying continued right into his sophomore year of high school.

"There were a lot of times I was hiding and running home from school," Greene said. "I was doing this because I was trying to avoid people that were dangerous to me, that wanted a piece of my hide. I can honestly say that I suffered from a complete lack of confidence on the field and in my personal life.

"I remember that I'd be looking out the door at the end of the school day to see if these people were out there looking for me. If I didn't see them, I'd just take off running all the way home. But the funny thing was, I wasn't fast, so they could catch me. I think the main reason I was bullied was because I was so big and they could brag that they took the big man down."

Greene said his main bully was actually a friend who was a couple year's older. Joe said that this guy was constantly teasing him and beating him up. He said it didn't matter when or where, the guy was constantly trying to get to him. But maybe the worst part for Joe was the fact that there were times when he acted like his friend.

A transformation occurred during his sophomore season when his friend/bully took five dollars that Joe's mom had left for him in the house. The money was to have been used to pay for the insurance that Greene needed to play on the high school football team.

"When I confronted him about the money, he admitted that he had taken it, and that's where the transformation occurred," recalled Greene. "What he did was unforgivable, so I attacked him and kept hitting him. For whatever reason, I overcame my fear right then. I went from being large and timid to being large and very aggressive. I took that and used it on the football field."

Even though Greene acknowledged that he knew he wasn't going to be a running back from the days of playing pick-up football games, when he tried out for the freshman football team, his coach decided that, because of Joe's size, he should be a fullback.

"Back then we were playing the single wing, and me and the other biggest guy on the team were in the backfield," Greene remembered. "I still remember the play, 26 Spinner. The quarterback would get the ball, turn his back, fake it to the fullback, then fake to the tailback, and then the deep back would spin around and get the ball.

"We played Austin Anderson, which was a pretty good football team in Class AAA. They just killed me. I never got out of the backfield. From a historical perspective, I'm glad that that was the last time I ever played fullback. I would never have made it if I had stayed in the backfield."

Greene credits his Dunbar High School head varsity coach Lester Moore for his development.

"Coach Moore was from the old school and talked a lot about physicality," said Greene. "He was always talking about being physical and being aggressive. One of his old-fashion sayings was, 'It's not the size of the dog, but the size of the fight in the dog.' He would say that saying just about every day. What that meant to me was that anybody could play the game, no matter what size you were, but what it really came down to was how much energy you put forth in doing what you were doing.

"Over time I believed that what I was doing on the field was brought about by anger. I did realize over time that the anger wasn't what was supposed to propel me—it should have been the competition."

Greene said that Coach Moore was all about out-hustling the other guy. He also had rules about no smoking, no drinking, and he didn't want to see you with a girl the day before a game. If you were caught breaking his rules, he would make you do rollovers, where you'd start at the goal line and keep rolling over and over and over until you were ready to throw up. Greene said that in most cases the player would throw up.

While Joe didn't get his nickname "Mean Joe" until his time at North Texas State, which is now the University of North Texas, he admits that he was definitely mean on the high school field.

"I was very immature," said Greene. "Our football team wasn't very good, and I hated losing. I'd hit opponents inappropriately and then I'd yell at the refs. I had a very bad attitude. And, as time went by, I started to get a reputation as a player who didn't mind taking someone out.

"There were moments back then that I'm not proud of. The penalties, getting kicked out of games. The truth of the matter is, I really didn't change my attitude until I got to the pros."

Green is very introspective now about his transformation from being bullied to becoming the guy that bullied people on the high school football field and then learning a better way. He said that because of his style of play back at Dunbar High, and the losses, he doesn't really have one specific game that stands out as he looks back on his time in Temple. He can't even recall the team's record but guessed that the team's best finish was 4–6.

"All of the tirades that I went through weren't of a selfish nature, because I wasn't thinking that it was all about me," Greene said. "It was the only way I knew how to compete and be a team player. Looking back, I thought some of the things I was doing made me a team player, but the fact is I wasn't being a team player. Chuck Noll was a great man, who taught me a different way from what I knew growing up."

The funny thing about Joe Greene is he's not real fond of his nickname "Mean Joe."

"It's not really who I am," he said. "Remember, when I was a kid I was scared and bullied. And, as I said before, I never liked the contact of football, but I did grow up to love the game itself and all that comes with it."

AFTER HIGH SCHOOL

Because Dunbar High School wasn't the best football team, Greene didn't get a lot of looks from colleges. He settled on North Texas State, where the "Mean Joe" nickname was born. During his three years as a starter, Greene led the team to a 23–5–1 record. After his outstanding senior season, he was named to the All-American Team.

The Pittsburgh Steelers selected Greene with the fourth overall pick in the 1969 NFL Draft. Despite the team's 1–13 record in 1969, Greene was named the NFL Defensive Rookie of the Year and first team All-Pro. After four Super Bowl championships, Greene retired after the 1981 season. In 1984, he was inducted into the College Football Hall of Fame and the Pro Football Hall of Fame three years later, in 1987.

Greene said his poor high school and college anger habits were still causing issues until Pittsburgh Steelers head coach Chuck Noll talked to him about making a change.

"As a man, as a coach, and a leader, Chuck exemplified what that meant to me," said Greene. "Remember, I hated losing and that played a role in me acting out starting in high school. My first year we were 1–13 with the Steelers, and I watched how he stayed the course. There were times when it was difficult to see a light at the end of the tunnel, but he would always talk about and teach you things that would lead us to success and winning.

"He would talk to me about officials when I was acting very unruly to them. He would say, 'Joe, these officials are human, they have families and people that love them, and I'm sure that they don't like the way you talk to them.' I thought about it as

I was walking away and it did settle in that I was being abusive. Chuck was a smart man who knew what buttons to push and that's when I realized that football, at every level from high school through college into the pros, is not about being aggressive, it is about the competition, about your teammates and your coaches."

9

Ken Houston—Dunbar High School— Lufkin, Texas

KEN HOUSTON HAD a Pro Football Hall of Fame career thanks to his desire for a date. Yes, Houston, who played for the Houston Oilers and Washington Redskins, was headed toward a basketball career until he wanted to ask a young lady out on a date before his sophomore year at Dunbar High School. During Houston's freshman year, he was actually a member of the school's marching band during football season.

"There was a girl that I liked, and I had to get out of the band to ask her out," chuckled Houston, who said he played in the band until his sophomore season. "I knew she wouldn't go out with me if I was in the band, but I thought she'd like me if I was a football player. I could only play about three notes anyway, so it didn't really matter if I left the band."

For those wondering, Houston didn't get the date he was hoping for, but he did get an incredible football career that took him to Canton.

"That's probably why I played angry," laughed Houston.

Kenneth Ray Houston was born on November 12, 1944, in Lufkin, Texas, the third of four children. He described his life as a boy in small-town Lufkin as very enjoyable.

"I had a great life outside of sports," said Houston. "I liked hiking and fishing and the Boys Scouts. As far as high school sports, we went from one to the other...football to basketball to track. I believe in kids playing more than one sport. I was a better basketball player than I was a football player, but each sport helped me with the other."

Houston played during segregation. Dunbar was the school attended by Lufkin's African Americans, and Lufkin High was for white residents in the East Texas town. Dunbar, which was closed in 1970 after desegregation, was part of the Prairie View Interscholastic League (PVIL), which was the counterpart of the University Interscholastic League (UIL), which excluded black schools from membership until 1967.

Like most players in the sixties, Houston was a two-way player. He was a center on offense and defensive tackle on defense.

"Mild-mannered is how I'd describe Ken back then," said Oscar Kennedy, whose father was a coach on the Dunbar staff when Houston was playing. "I was young, but I remember he was respectful saying 'Yes sir, no sir.'"

Houston played under the legendary Elmer Redd, who as head coach at Dunbar led the Tigers to two PVIL state championships in 1964 and 1967. When Lufkin consolidated its schools in 1970, Redd moved on to the University of Houston where he served as Bill Yeoman's running backs coach. Together, Redd and Yeoman developed the Veer Offense, which helped Houston become one of the top programs in the nation.

"Coach Redd was very dedicated to his players," recalled Houston. "He wanted to make sure you were in bed in the summertime. He kinda ran the town, especially for the kids in athletics. In our small town, he had more power than our parents in some cases. If he told you to go to bed, you went straight to bed.

"Elmer Redd had a 1954 green Cadillac, and when that car was driving up and down the street, he was like a gang boss to us kids. If we saw that car and we were supposed to be home, we would fly home! He really did care about us doing the right thing."

Houston fondly remembers how many times Coach Redd would come by his house in the country, driving the school bus to make sure that Ken and other players made it to the games.

"My parents were very strict," recalled Houston. "They were very religious, and back in those days, you would go home from school and then come back for practice or the games. I would get home, and my mom would say that I should stay home and relax and not worry about playing games. Then Coach Redd would come by driving the school bus and convince my mom that I needed to go to the game. Remember, we were a small school, and if I didn't show up they probably didn't have another center."

"I remember that well," said Oscar Kennedy, who became a coach in town (like his father) after his playing days. "I think all of the assistant coaches had pick-up trucks and sometimes you'd see a lot of kids in the back riding to practice on 'The Hill,' which was on the back of the campus where the practice field and field house were located. Even to this day, you'll hear people in the town talking about 'up on the hill.'

"As I look back on those days, Coach Redd and all of the coaches, including my father, were all about the kids. They had the kids' best interests at heart, and the parents in town knew that."

Now in his early seventies, Houston enjoys talking about his early life in Lufkin, rather than discussing the fact that he's considered one of the greatest defensive backs in NFL history. His HOF career includes twelve Pro Bowl appearances.

"Football really wasn't my life, it still isn't," said Houston. "I lived out in the country. That was life before football. After football, I went back to that life."

Because newspapers didn't cover the PVIL that much, many of its great players—like Houston and "Mean Joe" Greene—didn't get much notoriety.

Houston's brother Joseph, who was one year ahead of him in school, played on the same team. The two actually played the same position, and Ken started ahead of Joseph at center even though he was a year younger.

Because Dunbar shared the town's one high school football stadium with the all-white Lufkin High School, all of Dunbar's home games were played on Saturdays.

"You would have a ton of white people at Dunbar's games," recalled Oscar Kennedy. "They wanted to come to see a team that had very good athletes. And, you have to remember, in a town of 30,000 people you know everybody. The Dunbar coaches went out and interacted with everyone, asking for support for the team by making friends."

While Dunbar wasn't a big school, graduating about sixty students a year, its football team had big names. Houston estimates that about thirty-five kids played on the football team. Aside from Houston, four other players from his team played in the NFL: defensive tackle Finus Taylor with the Oakland Raiders, running back Joseph Harold Williams played with the Dallas Cowboys (1971–1972), Clifford Brooks played with the Cleveland Browns (1972–1974, and with other teams from 1975–1976), and Tommy B. Davis played with the Baltimore Colts.

"Can you believe it?" asked Houston. "Five of us seniors (Class of 1962) from that team of thirty-five players made it to the NFL. Isn't that amazing?"

Despite all of that talent, Houston said that his team never got a shot at playing for a state title.

"You gotta remember that many of the black schools had outstanding talent," stated Houston. "Back then, Baytown Carver High and Corpus Christi Coles High School were very good with plenty of players that went on to the NFL. They were always beating us out.

"We didn't play high school football with any intent," he continued. "We didn't play it with the intent to get a scholarship. We didn't play it for the intent of attaining glory. We played high school football because it was the thing to do in a small town."

AFTER HIGH SCHOOL

Prairie View A&M College (now Prairie View A&M University) was the only school to recruit Houston out of high school.

"Prairie View really liked me, but they weren't recruiting me," said Houston. "We [Dunbar] had an offensive tackle named Wiley Smith that Prairie View really wanted. Looking back, they took me in order to get him."

Houston started out as a center but was then moved to linebacker where he became an All-American in the Southwestern Athletic Conference.

The Houston Oilers drafted Houston in the ninth round of the AFL-NFL Draft in 1967. He played with the Oilers until 1972, when he was traded to the Washington Redskins. Houston intercepted 49 passes in his career and recovered 21 fumbles.

After his retirement, Houston became a counselor in the Houston Independent School District, where he also coached high school football. He was the head coach at Houston Wheatley High and Westbury High School.

"I really enjoyed coaching the kids," said Houston, who was an assistant coach for several years with the Oilers after his retirement. "I was always about the kids."

10

Craig James—Stratford High School— Houston, Texas

FOUR DECADES SINCE winning a Texas high school football championship, Craig James feels like he and his Stratford High School teammates still don't get the recognition they deserve.

Jesse Craig James was born on January 2, 1961, in Jacksonville, Texas. At a young age, after his parents divorced, James moved to Pasadena, Texas, with his mother.

James said it seems like comparing apples and oranges, but he truly would rather play one more year with his high school team than any other squad that he's been a part of, which includes his college and pro teams.

"If the Lord said, 'Craig, if you can go back and play one more season what would it be?' My answer without hesitation would be that I would want to go back to play on that 1978 championship team again," said James. "That team was better than the conference championship teams I played on at SMU (1981 and 1982), it was better than my Super Bowl team (1985) with the Patriots. That's if we made it apples to apples. We were just a *really* good team."

That's a pretty big statement for anyone to make, but James said it with such sincerity that you know that it's true. His heart is still a Stratford Spartan.

That Stratford team was tight, according to James. Maybe it was the fact that the school had just opened a few years earlier, or maybe it was just that his teammates believed in a goal that was set for them as sophomores.

"We worked for each other and together," James said. "Oscar Cripps, our head coach, had a saying, 'It's amazing how much can be accomplished when no one cares who gets the credit.' I think we bought into that as sophomores. We bought into our 'State in '78' campaign. We had a lot of hard workers. We put in the grind hours, and we were committed to sacrificing to prepare…whatever that meant. We were all in."

And, in true share the credit form, James quickly began to name teammates who were integral to a juggernaut offense that scored 532 points that season, which was the second-highest total ever scored in Class 4A (which was then the state's largest classification, now known as Class 6A).

The State in '78 slogan came from a poster that was created by Stratford's JV sophomore team in 1976. That poster was signed by James and all the members of that sophomore team and hung above the team's locker room door.

"We had a great sophomore team in 1976, which was the foundation for the state championship team," said James. "We didn't keep stats, but I remember running for hundreds of yards a game. However, the funniest thing about those yards was the fact that because I was the team's kicker I wore the old-school square toe on my right foot and I never changed my shoe. I would score a touchdown and then stay on the field and kick the extra point without changing my shoe. It was awesome!"

Counting James, nine players from that 1978 squad went on to play Division I-A college football, with three others playing college football for smaller schools. Like James, lineman Chuck Thomas made it all the way to the pros, playing on two Super Bowl teams for the San Francisco 49ers.

Jim May was an offensive tackle on the '78 team, who stays in touch with many of his Stratford teammates. He added that '78 is still a bonding moment for his teammates, recalling that "Just the other night, six of us from the Dallas-Forth Worth area got together for dinner, and that happens fairly regularly and always the conversation slips back to that season, which was a once in a lifetime deal. Basically, most of us grew up from seventh grade on and knew everything about each other and loved each other. It really was some sixty-three or so close friends. It was just a whole lot of fun!"

"Our quarterback was Mark Gabrisch," said James. "I played with a pretty good option quarterback at SMU [Lance McIlhenny from Highland Park High School in Texas], but Mark was every bit as good. He had that *it* factor. He had the ability to run it, to throw it. He had the poise and charisma. Most importantly, he had the poise to handle our offensive coordinator Bob French, who was really demanding."

James said the blend of head coach Oscar Cripps and Bob French were perfect because they were so different, but both were all about the kids.

"The hallmark for [head coach] Oscar Cripps was he treated everyone the same...whether you were a starter or just someone who was just trying to put the shoulder pads on right," said James. "He loved everyone. His perspective wasn't just football. He genuinely cared about mentoring us as people...as young teenagers. That's sometimes hard to find in a coach. And, to this day, many of us are believers in Jesus Christ because of Coach Cripps and his influence on us.

"And then we had the hard, gruff offensive coordinator Bob French. I give him all of the credit for pushing me beyond my comfort zones. He was very demanding of me personally. I know now that he saw potential in me. Because of that, on my non-carry plays, he demanded that I be an excellent blocker, requiring excellence in every phase of the game."

"It was the perfect yin and yang situation when it came to those two coaches," May said. "Coach Cripps was the pious, spiritual, steady, never raised his voice, calming presence. Coach French was the cursing, loud, yelling, push you up against the chalkboard guy. When that whip needed to be pulled out, he was the guy to do it.

"But here's the thing about Coach French, as tough as he was, he is to this day, including my time playing four years at Baylor, one of the smartest offensive minds that I've ever been around. That guy knew offense and how to dissect a defense as good as any college coach I had ever been around."

French was also James's baseball coach. Craig was an excellent baseball player, who was offered $125,000 in high school to sign a Major League Baseball contract with the Philadelphia Phillies. James's younger brother Chris had a ten-year career in the majors as a utility player for eight different teams.

"Here's the beauty of Bob French, he knew the buttons to push," James said pointedly. "I think sometime during my junior year of football I was considered a blue chip, but French told me that the college coaches that were interested in me said that I didn't break enough tackles and make enough yards on my own. I don't know if they actually said it, but by Bob saying that it really motivated me because I was scared.

"That lit a fire under my fanny so that in the offseason I worked hard to get more physical. I was looking for a way out. I wanted to go to college."

"We didn't even know what Craig was heading into our senior season," said May. "He was a bit of a late bloomer physically. He probably put on 20 to 30 pounds between our junior and senior years. We knew he was going to be good, but 2,400 yards good? Craig was as humble then as he is now."

To say Craig James was good in 1978 would be an understatement. James broke Earl Campbell's single season Class 4A rushing record of 2,036 yards. Check that, he destroyed it by rushing for 2,411 yards. Making that number even more amazing was that James recalled that he only carried the ball between 13 to 15 times a game. It wasn't just James amassing chunks of yardage out of the Spartans' wishbone formation. Stratford as a team rushed for over 7,000 yards in 1978.

"When I broke the record against Churchill, I remember it being up on the Astrodome scoreboard in big numbers," recalled James. "I remember looking up at it, thinking to myself WOW! I kept the football, and I'm looking at it right now on my mantle in my study as I talk with you. But here's the thing, everyone on the offense was pumped for us to get that record."

"Out of all of the people that had the right to, as Cripps would say, 'Get the big head,' it was Craig, but he stayed humble," said Jim May. "Every interview during the year he would thank 'his guys.' He never took credit for anything, and he's still that same way to this day."

"In a time that was way pre-Internet, I don't think anyone on the team was really aware of the record until the San Antonio Churchill game in the state semifinals. When I heard it, I remember thinking that that's a lot of yards!"

The 24–7 win over Churchill marked the second time that season that Stratford defeated a recent state champion. Churchill was the 1976 state champ. During the regular season, the Spartans beat 1975 state champ Port Neches-Groves.

Like the state semifinal game, the 4A state championship game was played in the Astrodome, which gave Stratford a huge home-field advantage. The Spartans' opponent was defending 1977 Class 4A champ Plano.

"That state championship game was a lot of fun," James said. "I remember there was a big crowd in the Dome and the celebration."

James and company didn't disappoint the crowd of nearly 30,000, which included a large contingent of Spartan fans. Stratford held a 13–7 halftime lead on a 46-yard touchdown pass from Gabrisch to James and an 11-yard touchdown run by James. His 80-yard TD run in the third quarter blew the game open, and Stratford celebrated the title with a 29–13 victory. James finished with 168 yards on just 13 carries.

As far as the question of why Stratford isn't mentioned in the same breath as the all-time great teams like Tyler's John Tyler High with Earl Campbell or the 1985 Houston Yates High School team, we'll leave that to those that like to debate such things. But as far as James and his teammates are concerned, Stratford needs to be in the conversation, which usually isn't the case.

"What a team," said James. "Our numbers and accomplishments that year speak volumes of our place in Texas high school football history. Almost all of our starters went on to play college football. Also, you have to remember that the 1978 success continues to this day, because all of us have become personally responsible, good, solid producing citizens throughout life who are good family men with faith, and *that* is the ultimate in success."

AFTER HIGH SCHOOL

James attended Southern Methodist University because his girlfriend and future wife Marylyn was already enrolled at the university. The Mustangs had a long championship dry spell before James arrived in the same recruiting class with Eric Dickerson from Sealy, Texas. The two became known as "The Pony Express," leading SMU, which hadn't won a Southwest Conference championship since 1948, to two conference championships in 1981 and 1982.

After college, the Washington Federals of the United States Football League (USFL) drafted James, who decided to sign with the upstart league instead of waiting for the 1983 NFL Draft (which was a few days later). Even though he was already playing with the Federals, the New England Patriots drafted the rights to James in the seventh round of the NFL Draft. The Patriots' head coach at that time was Ron Meyer, who was James' head coach at SMU.

James played two years in the cash-strapped USFL before being released for financial reasons. He then signed with the Patriots. When the aforementioned Raymond Berry took over as the head coach of the Patriots in 1985, he installed James as the team's starting running back where James gained 1,227 yards, leading the Pats to Super Bowl XX that they lost to the Chicago Bears. James was named to the Pro Bowl that year. He retired in 1988 because of a series of injuries.

11

Bob Lilly—Throckmorton High School—Throckmorton, Texas

WHILE BOB LILLY is known as "Mr. Cowboy," did you know that the man who played his entire career with the Dallas Cowboys played his final high school football games in the state of Oregon? Lilly's parents moved the family to Pendleton, Oregon, because of the extended Texas drought in the 1950s. They landed in Pendleton because the Lilly's had family there and could easily land jobs.

"We packed up and left," said Lilly in his book *A Cowboys Life*.

Robert Lewis Lilly was born on July 26, 1939, in the tiny town of Olney, Texas, which as of 2017 has a population just above 3,000. However, Lilly grew up in another small town, Throckmorton, which currently has a population of fewer than 1,000 residents and is located about two hours northwest of the Dallas-Fort Worth Metroplex.

He began playing youth football in Throckmorton, but Lilly, who was a tall, skinny kid, also played basketball and volleyball in high school. Lilly got his first chance to play with the Throckmorton High School Greyhounds when he was a freshman. It was in high school where he began to put on weight and grow into the big defensive lineman who would later be inducted into both the College and Pro Football Hall of Fames. Lilly grew from 5-foot-8 as an eighth grader to 6-foot-4 as a sophomore.

During Lilly's junior year, he was spotlighted as one of Throckmorton's top returners from a 5–4 team in 1954 in the *Abilene Reporter-News'* preseason story on the Greyhound football team. Throckmorton would finish 4–5 in Lilly's final high school football season in Texas. Newspaper recaps from that season mentioned that Lilly blocked a punt and caught a touchdown pass in a 51–0 win over Roby during the Greyhounds' Homecoming Game. He then caught a pass in his final Texas high school football game against Merkel. Lilly caught the ball and fumbled it as he crossed the goal line, but his center Butch Timms recovered it for the game-winning score in a 12–7 victory.

After his junior season, Lilly was voted All-District and All-Bi-District in both football and basketball. He averaged 27 points per game as a basketball player and was a state high school javelin champ as a junior.

"Playing football at Throckmorton was routine for me," said Lilly via email correspondence. "My more meaningful year was when I lived in Pendleton, Oregon, and of course, when I played for the Cowboys."

The Lilly's first settled in Hermiston when they arrived in Oregon, but it wasn't long before the hard-to-miss seventeen-year-old caught the eye of legendary Pendleton head football coach Don Requa. Pendleton is about 35 miles southeast of Hermiston in the northeast part of the state.

Requa, who won 301 high school football games in 41 years as a head coach, took over the Buckaroos' football program in 1950. According to Tom Melton, who is the President of the Pendleton Linebacker's Club Hall of Fame, Coach Requa, who passed away in the late '80s, immediately wanted to know who the new tall kid was as soon as he saw him in the nearby town of Hermiston.

"The myth here is that Coach Requa happened to be at a party in Hermiston and asked the Hermiston coach about this big kid he saw," recalled Melton, who has interviewed Lilly six or seven times for his Pendleton's Hall of Fame induction ceremony. "Supposedly, the Hermiston coach told Requa that he was a new kid from Texas and his dad was looking for a job.

"However, Hermiston definitely believes that we [Pendleton] got Bob's dad a job and we ended up with one of the greatest players in the history of football," Melton added with a chuckle. "Yes, they believe we stole him."

Lilly said he doesn't recall the story that way but doesn't discount that it could be true.

Melton, who was around five years old at the time Lilly played for the Buckaroos, said he's too young to remember seeing him play, but he did talk with Coach Requa a lot about the future HOFer. While the true story of how Mr. Cowboy ended-up in Pendleton over Hermiston may be in question, what isn't a myth is that Coach Requa told Melton that he absolutely adored Bob.

"Req [Coach Requa's nickname] used to love talking about what a wonderful guy Bob was, as much as he was an incredible player," said Melton. "Coach would tell the story after Lilly's first practice that he couldn't believe how Bob could run. He weighed about 215 at the time, but he still ran a 4.6 or 4.7 40-yard dash. Coach would always tell me that Bob had a sixth sense on the football field, which led to him being double- and triple-teamed. Req said he had freakish ability, freakish smarts, and a great memory."

While Lilly only spent about nine months in Pendleton before going back to Texas to start his college career at Texas Christian University, his impact on the community and his teammates was very strong and carries through to this day.

"The guys in Pendleton immediately fell in love with him," said Melton. "He was just one of the guys, and that's the way he's lived his life. His attachment to his Buckaroo teammates is still legendary in Pendleton."

Surprisingly, one of Lilly's Pendleton teammates, Gerald Ayler, was also from Texas. Ayler, who was inducted into the Pendleton Hall of Fame in 2017, grew up in the Texas panhandle where he spent time living in Borger, Amarillo, and Lubbock before moving with his family to Oregon when he was thirteen years old.

Ayler recalls that when Lilly moved to town, some residents told Bob that there was another kid from Texas attending Pendleton High.

"The story goes that when Bob asked people at the school what my name was they really weren't quite sure, and then someone said it's Gerald Ayler," recalled Ayler, who was a running back and linebacker for the Pendleton Buckeroos. "That's when Bob said, 'Why don't we just call him Tex?' It stuck, and to this day, I'm known as Tex Ayler."

That's not the only thing that stuck. Lilly and Ayler have been friends ever since. When Ayler was inducted into the Pendleton Linebacker's Club Hall of Fame in 2017, Lilly attended the ceremony for the man he dubbed Tex.

"Bob just bloomed when he came to Pendleton," Ayler said. "Now, Bob was a big lineman, we both played both ways, but I remember every once in a while, we'd put him at end. He was so tall, my gosh, we figured we'd just toss him the ball and, when Bob fell down, we'd be close to picking up ten yards and a first down. We'd just lob the ball to him and he'd just stretch out those long arms."

As far as their sixty-year friendship, Ayler says that it's simply planted in their roots, meaning they both grew up in the Lone Star State.

"We loved to just talk about those days in Texas," recalled Ayler. "We'd talk about how everything where we grew up was brown or shades of brown, because we had so much dust in our towns. Then we got to Oregon, and everything was so green, so clear, and you could see forever. We were always comparing notes on how things were when we grew up in Texas and what they were like now when we got here."

The other thing I remember is I could always make Bob laugh so easily," Ayler added. "He would just crack-up with some of the things I'd come up with."

Another one of Lilly's Buckeroo teammates was Dick Bunch, who was a junior when Bob was a senior. Bunch, who had played quarterback his entire career, was shifted to a receiver for the 1956 season.

"I remember that after [Coach] Req switched me from quarterback, I realized that I'd have to go up against Bob during a one-on-one drill in practice," recalled Bunch. "He beat me up pretty badly three or four times, and I think Coach, who we called Old Blood and Guts, felt sorry for me. After that, they moved Bob to tackle on offense instead of end. I guess I became an end by default.

"We had some good players and a good team, but we just couldn't get over the top. When we saw Bob on the practice field, we knew that he was something special and might be able to help us a lot."

And help he did, as Pendleton finished 7–1–1, winning the Blue Mountain League with a perfect 4–0 league record and a district championship. The Buckaroos entered the playoffs ranked No. 6 in the state in the Associated Press rankings.

Pendleton opened the Class A-1 playoffs with a 25–6 win over Albany, ranked No. 9 in the state, in the quarterfinals. The Buckaroos used a punishing ground game led by Lilly, who was named second team All-State that year, and his offensive line teammates to beat the Bulldogs. Newspaper reports about the game indicate that Lilly and his teammates dominated throughout with 252 yards rushing.

The Albany win sent Pendleton into the state semifinals against defending state champ Marshfield High School, which was ranked No. 1 in the state. That's where the season ended for Pendleton with a 32–14 defeat. Bunch pointed out that the outcome may have been a lot different if Pendleton hadn't had four touchdowns called back on penalties.

"Years later, a writer for the *Oregonian* told me that was the best football game he had ever watched. Whenever Bob and I get together, we always replay that game," chuckled Bunch.

Bunch's wife Anne said, "The one thing that people need to know about Bob is he was a gentleman back then and remains that to this day. Through all of the celebrity, he's the same guy that he was in Pendleton."

"I just idolize the guy," said Dick Bunch.

AFTER HIGH SCHOOL

Lilly returned to the Lone Star State to play his college ball at Texas Christian University. During his senior season at TCU, he was named an All-American.

Lilly was taken 13th overall by the Dallas Cowboys in the 1961 NFL Draft. He was also drafted in the second round of the 1961 American Football League Draft by the Dallas Texas, who would become the Kansas City Chiefs. Lilly would be named an All-Pro seven times in his career, and he was elected to the Pro Football Hall of Fame in 1980 and the College Football Hall of Fame in 1981.

12

Andrew Luck—Stratford High School— Houston, Texas

YOU COULD SAY that being a quarterback is the Luck family business.

Andrew Austen Luck was born on September 12, 1989, to Oliver and Kathy Luck in Washington, DC. Luck's father, who is currently in charge of the National Collegiate Athletic Association's (NCAA) regulatory functions, played five seasons in the NFL as a quarterback for the Houston Oilers.

While born in Washington, DC, Andrew spent a lot of his early years overseas because his father was the general manager of the Frankfurt Galaxy and Rhein Fire football teams in the World League of American Football. Luck attended grade school at the Frankfurt International School in Frankfurt, Germany. The Luck's returned to America when Oliver was named chief executive officer of the Harris County-Houston Sports Authority.

Kathy Luck said Andrew began attending games when he was two years old and her husband was working in Europe. Because American football was in its fledgling stage overseas, Andrew began playing the other football…the one that is spelled with a "u," or soccer as it's known stateside. However, once the Luck family returned to the states when Andrew was around nine years old, he turned his attention to the game that he loved watching at an extremely young age.

With great DNA, Andrew's focus was on being a quarterback, but he was also an excellent student at Stratford High School, the same school where the aforementioned Craig James was a star in 1978.

"My high school days are a great part of my football memories, both on and off the field," said Luck when I interviewed him in 2012 at the Maxwell Football Club awards dinner. "The classroom was always an important part of my life at Stratford because education opens so many doors."

In middle school, Luck played in an offense that didn't throw a lot, but when he attended Stratford's freshman camp, the school's head coach Eliot Allen knew that he had a guy who could wing it.

"Quite honestly, he [Luck] probably could have started as a freshman," said Allen. "His arm strength was always great, but what was more important to me with him was his accuracy and throwing catchable balls. At the high school level, you have receivers with different levels of talent and what amazed me about Andrew was that when he was looking at his receiver, he would know what type of ball to throw to match the receiver's abilities. That is very impressive."

Luck's freshman season was cut short by a broken collarbone, but Allen said he was impressive enough to know that he would be able to challenge for the starting QB job as a sophomore, a rarity in Texas high school football. Luck became a varsity starter at Stratford during his sophomore year with the Spartans going 5–5, but Allen said that it could have been a better year if he hadn't limited the playbook.

"He had decent size, but we weren't really sure what we had, especially since our program always relies on seniors," said Allen. "We weren't sure what he could handle, so we didn't want to give him too much. Everything we threw at him, he not only understood it, but he also understood why we were doing it. It just amazed me at what a great football mind he had."

Sam Kahn, a high school sports writer for the *Houston Chronicle*, said that Luck was one of those once-in-a-lifetime players, "The thing that sticks out to me, and I always tell people about covering Andrew Luck, is that was the first time as a high school reporter that I saw a guy on the field and I thought to myself that that guy's going to play on Sunday.

"Andrew was just a different kid from the rest of the athletes. When he told you that academics were important, you knew that he meant it. Even when I see him in interviews today, he's more mature, but his disposition is still the same as the one he had during his Stratford days."

The national spotlight began shining on Luck during his junior year when he threw for 2,926, which nearly doubled his sophomore numbers. He also threw 27 touchdowns. His standout season led Stratford to a district championship and his first post-season appearance, as well as the Spartans' first playoff appearance in thirteen years. After a 35–16 win over Chavez in the opening round of the Class 5A Division II playoffs, the Spartans moved on to play Cypress Falls in the second round for a game that Luck remembers as one of his best high school football memories.

Cy Fair was loaded with talent, led by junior running back Sam McGuffie, who ran for over 3,100 yards that season with 44 touchdowns. McGuffie would go on to play as a true freshman at the University of Michigan before transferring to Rice.

The game was quintessential Andrew Luck, with him attacking the Eagles with his arm and his legs. Stratford jumped out to a 20–7 halftime lead against Cy Falls by scoring on all three of its first-half offensive possessions.

"Andrew was playing extremely well in that first half," said Kahn, who now covers college football and basketball for ESPN .com. "Cy Falls' defense really started getting to Luck in the second half and it became a classic Texas high school football battle."

Cy Falls outscored Stratford 27–7 in the second half. Then with 1:52 to go in the game, Cy Falls took a 34–27 lead. Luck and the Spartans roared back with Andrew tossing a 42-yard touchdown pass to John Sorsby to cut the Cy Falls lead to 34–33 with 55 seconds to play. All Stratford had to do was kick the extra point, but the Eagles' Stedmann Coleman blocked the PAT.

Believe it or not, Stratford got the ball back to give Luck and the Spartans one more shot at moving on to the third round of the playoffs. Unfortunately, Luck's Hail Mary heave into the end zone with no time left was intercepted.

"That's one of those games you'd like to have back," said Luck six years after the final horn sounded. "We gave it our all, but it didn't take away from what a great season it was for my teammates and me."

"If we didn't have Andrew Luck, we would not have had a shot at that game at the end," said Allen about the Hail Mary. "Everyone knew what we were going to do at the end, and he was able to throw it so accurately that we had a shot at it."

• • •

Luck finished the game completing 17-of-28 passes for 339 yards with four touchdowns. He also gained 91 yards with his legs, even though he was sacked five times.

"The thing that I remember the most about that game was a play that didn't even count," recalled Kahn. "It was in the third quarter, and he's rolling to his right, and just before he's chased out of bounds, he just flings it out and the ball ends up in his receiver's arms about 50 yards down the field. It was called back on a penalty, but me and some other reporters in the press box jumped up because of what we just saw."

Allen said he also remembers that throw as well, but more because he didn't like the penalty call.

With nearly every big-time college football team in the nation vying for Luck's services, he led his teammates three rounds deep into the postseason during his senior season, finishing a

9–4 season with a 31–27 loss to Fort Bend Clements in the state quarterfinals.

"Nothing really matches your time playing high school football with your friends and teammates," recalled Luck. "We did some really great things on that team, which will stay with me the rest of my life."

"Not only was he a phenomenal football player, but he was an even better person off the field," said Allen. "He was ranked No. 1 in his class and was an outstanding person in the community. He was a great leader. He was the first one at practice and the last to leave."

How much did Luck enjoy his high school days? Instead of just signing his name on his Indianapolis Colts jersey that hangs in the school's main office, he signed it with "Spartan Pride."

AFTER HIGH SCHOOL

With education being important to Luck, he headed west to play his college football at Stanford where he became a two-time All-American. He finished runner-up in the Heisman voting in 2010 and 2011.

The Indianapolis Colts drafted Luck as the overall No. 1 pick in the 2012 NFL Draft. In his first three seasons as a pro, he led the Colts to three straight playoff appearances, winning the AFC's South Division twice.

13

Don Maynard—Colorado City High School—Colorado City, Texas

AT EIGHTY-THREE YEARS old, Pro Football Hall of Fame wide receiver Don Maynard still chuckles at the difference between the tiny Texas towns he lived in compared to his first trip to New York City. He began his career with the New York Giants before moving on to being an All-Pro receiver for the New York Jets and its celebrity quarterback Joe Namath.

"I remember getting off a bus for the first time in New York City, and I looked up and saw more bricks in one building than some of the entire towns that I lived in growing up," said Maynard in his thick Texas drawl.

Donald Rogers Maynard was born on January 25, 1935, in the small town of Crosbyton, Texas, which according to the 2010 census has a total 1,741 residents, located east of Lubbock. Maynard recalled that his childhood was filled with plenty of moving around.

"My dad worked in the cotton business, running a cotton gin that he managed," recalled Maynard. "My dad was very influential in my life. We moved a lot. I think I went to thirteen different schools."

Maynard said his dad was a very hard worker and never actually saw his son play football until he was a junior in college at Texas Western University, which is now the University of Texas at El Paso, otherwise known as UTEP.

From as far back as Maynard can remember, he was always the fastest kid in whatever community he lived in.

"I really loved running track," said Maynard. "I loved to run, and that helped me playing football. I remember playing games with my friends in the neighborhood on vacant lots."

When it was time to go to high school, the Maynard's lived in a rural area about 50 miles west of Lubbock. Maynard attended the Three Way Independent School District, which was named that because it combined three independent school districts into one, but Maynard said there were actually five little schools in the district. At one point, the district encompassed an amazing 352 square miles.

Maynard said getting to school was a chore unto itself. "I lived 13 miles from the school, but the way the bus route was going home, it was very roundabout, and I think my ride was about twenty-five miles."

The Three Way School was a six-man high school football team when Maynard began playing varsity football. For those unfamiliar with six-man football, it was created during the Great Depression in 1934 in Nebraska as an alternative for schools that didn't have enough students to play the eleven-man game. Colorado, Kansas, Montana, Nebraska, Oklahoma, Oregon, and Texas still offer six-man football, which is played on a field that is 80 yards long and 40 yards wide. All six players are eligible receivers in the scaled-down version of the game.

"I think back then we had about ten players on the team," said Maynard. "Of course, back then you played both ways. I think I played a little quarterback then, but mostly I was a halfback. To be honest, I don't remember much about the actual games, but I do remember I loved playing football."

For his junior season in 1951, Maynard and his family moved to Colorado City (with a population of around 4,000), which was a little bit bigger than Don was used to.

"I really enjoyed my time at Colorado (pronounced kol-*uh*-raid-oh)," said Maynard. "I remember playing football, basketball, and running track. But I've got to be honest with you, my state championships in the low and high hurdles stand out more than what I did on the football field."

Many called Maynard a one-man track team because, aside from the individual and relay running events, he was very good in the long and broad jumps.

As far as on the football field in 1952, Maynard played half-back in Colorado's Wing-T offense and a cornerback/safety on defense. He said he especially loved the defensive side of the ball.

"My claim to fame in high school was defense," said Maynard. "I would just sit back there and I was kind of tall, which together with my ability to read a formation made me a pretty good player. Knowing which way the other team was going to go out of different formations allowed me to pursue a ball carrier or knock down a pass.

"I like to think that the fact that I was fast made all of the difference in the world," Maynard added. "And if you're a good listener and pay attention, you can be a pretty good player. I believe I learned the game very well."

Maynard's best game may have been against Winters High School, nicknamed the Blizzards, in early October. He began the game with a 75-yard kickoff return for a touchdown. The speedy tailback then had an 81-yard catch and carry to tie the game at the half, 14–14. Maynard then capped the game with his third touchdown on a one-yard run, which gave Colorado City a 21–20 win after the extra point.

The 1952 football season ended with Colorado City beating Merkel, 12–7, which gave the Wolves a 5–5 record without a playoff berth. Maynard said he remembered that final game because he was named Wolverine Sweetheart, along with a young lady who was named Sweetheart of the Team. Capping the season was Maynard's selection to the District 5-AA All-District Team.

In the spring of his senior season, Maynard put his outstanding speed to work in the University Interscholastic League's Class A state track and field championships, winning the 180-yard low hurdles in a record time of 19.4 seconds. He also captured gold in the 120-yard high hurdles.

AFTER HIGH SCHOOL

After high school, Maynard headed to Rice Institute, now Rice University, but didn't enjoy his time in the Houston area.

"I think I came home five times during the first semester, and I didn't come home to visit, I came home to stay," chuckled Maynard. "But my dad said that I needed to get an education. So I went back all of those times and finally transferred to Texas Western, which is now the University of Texas at El Paso. The good thing was that in El Paso I got a roommate from high school, so that worked out real well."

At UTEP, Maynard continued to show his all-around skills on the football field. He only caught 28 passes there but averaged 27.6 yards per catch with ten touchdowns. As a running back, Maynard averaged 5.4 yards per carry. He finished his career with 2,283 all-purpose yards, which included his outstanding kickoff and punt returning skills. He also continued to perform well in the defensive secondary with 10 career interceptions.

Maynard was selected in the ninth round of the 1957 NFL Draft by the New York Giants but was released after only one year with the team. After an unsuccessful stint in the Canadian Football League, he signed with the New York Titans of the upstart American Football League. The Titans would be renamed the New York Jets several years later. In 1965, Maynard and "Broadway Joe" Namath began a pitch-and-catch relationship that would culminate with the Jets upsetting Baltimore in Super

Bowl III, 16–7, which marked the first time that an AFL team beat an NFL team in the Super Bowl.

In the end, Maynard retired as the NFL's all-time leading receiver with 633 receptions for an average of 18.7-yards per catch. He no longer holds the record, but he was inducted into the Pro Football Hall of Fame in 1987.

14

Mike Singletary—Worthing High School—Houston, Texas

FIVE.

That's the number of helmets that Mike Singletary broke during practices at Worthing High School in Houston. However, despite such power, Singletary was considered too small to play college football. He didn't get a lot of offers until accepting a scholarship to Baylor.

What might stand out more than his talent on the football field are the life lessons he learned from his high school football coach. Lessons that led him to become an assistant coach in the NFL with the Baltimore Ravens and San Francisco 49ers, where he eventually became the Niners' head coach.

Michael Singletary was born on October 9, 1958, in Houston, the youngest of ten children. Singletary said his relationship with his father eventually fell apart, which led to his brother Grady assuming the father figure role in the family until he was killed by a drunk driver in an automobile accident.

Singletary said his father was a Pentecostal minister who didn't believe in sports. "All of my brothers who were bigger than me and better than me didn't get to play."

He recalled the fact that his brothers not being allowed to play at Worthing High wasn't lost on the school's defensive coordinator Oliver Brown, who was a great coach in both football and track.

"When I first met Coach Brown," recalled Singletary, "he said 'You're one of those Singletary's, aren't you?' I said, 'Yes sir, I am.' So basically he's thinking, okay, it's another one of *those* Singletary's. But I told him *I* was going to play football.

"Being a kid from a broken home, dad left home when I was twelve, I was really trying to figure out my identity," Singletary continued. "It was a tough time trying to figure out who I was and where I was going to go. At that time, I was hanging out with a group of kids and needed to change directions. I needed to do a lot of things differently. My dad kind of started working with me…and dad could be tough, but he didn't finish. When he and my mom divorced, I was just kind of there."

Singletary said he went through middle school and had some "bumps and bruises" there, but when he got to high school,

Coach Brown began to have a big impact on his life that could have gone in many directions.

"He [Coach Brown] walked up to me on the first day and said, 'Son, I want you to understand something, you come out here to play this game, you gotta have your mind right…you gotta be focused…you gotta be a great student and you gotta have the character that people can look up to,'" recalled Singletary.

Singletary said that at the time, he really didn't understand what his coach was saying to him. He said that, in many ways, it was the same thing his parents had told him, but it was in a different way that he had never heard before. It was at that point that Mike began taking notice of the way his coach handled himself.

"He was tough," said Singletary. "He had a board in practice. If you didn't know what you were doing, you got popped on your tail. You had to know where you were going and what you were doing at all times.

"The thing about Coach Brown that I noticed more than anything else is about how he cared about the kids there," Singletary added. "How he cared about the community. How he made a difference in the community. There were kids that would come in and out of his office and they had issues. He knew every one of those kids…he even knew the kids that *didn't* play football. It was important to him that he knew about the lives of the kids, and today that's something I'm not sure is happening."

Singletary believes that the coaches from high school to college aren't really invested in the kids. He said one of his favorite stories about legendary coach Paul "Bear" Bryant was that he always did what was best for the kids.

"The one thing I know about Coach Brown is he was consistent," said Singletary. "To me, the 'C' in Coach stands for consistency. He must be the same guy every day."

As far as on the field, Singletary began playing middle linebacker in junior high but also enjoyed and excelled on the offensive line as a guard. He said he really loved the trap play because he loved getting to the linebacker, who had no clue where he was coming from.

During his induction into Pro Football's Hall of Fame, Singletary said that Willie Lanier, a fellow member of the HOF, was one of his idols. He said he could still remember thinking to himself, "I like the way he hits, and I like the way he brings it to the house."

Singletary played three seasons at Worthing High School, improving each year. The football field was the perfect outlet for Singletary to take out his aggressions that may have been caused by his tough family life. From his middle linebacker position, Singletary stalked ball carriers and receivers from sideline to sideline, from 1974 through 1976.

"I loved the freedom to be able to make a play anywhere at any time, as long as I was willing to hustle to get there," Singletary said. "Being a middle linebacker, I was able to see the ball and work on my vision and technique and mechanics. I was in a position where I could dictate where the defense was moving. I was going to put the defense in the best position."

Singletary was inducted into the Texas High School Football Hall of Fame in 2015.

AFTER HIGH SCHOOL

Singletary attended Baylor University where he became a two-time All-American linebacker in 1979 and 1980, averaging 10 tackles per game. The Chicago Bears drafted him with the 38th pick in the second round of the 1981 NFL Draft. He became a starter in the eighth game of his rookie season and played for Chicago his entire career, from 1981–1992. Singletary was known for his intensity and became the heart of the Bears defense which led them to a Super Bowl win in 1985. Singletary was elected to the Pro Football Hall of Fame in 1998.

After his playing days, Singletary went into coaching as a linebackers coach for the Baltimore Ravens. He moved on to the San Francisco 49ers where he was elevated to head coach in 2008 after Mike Nolan was fired. He served as the Niners' head coach until late into the 2010 regular season.

In March 2017, Singletary returned to his high school roots when he was named head coach at Trinity Christian School in Addison, Texas. At the time of his hiring, Singletary was quoted as saying, "Being able to coach Texas high school football, being able to coach at a Christian school, I may not get this chance again."

15

Lovie Smith—Big Sandy High School—Big Sandy, Texas

BIG SANDY IS a small East Texas town that did big things in the early '70s. The Big Sandy Wildcats were the center of attention in a town of about 1,000 residents, winning three straight Texas high school football championships. The team that won the third title in 1975 may go down as one of the best ever—not only in Texas but the entire country.

The 1975 squad featured former NFL head coach Lovie Smith and a future NFL first-round draft pick in David Overstreet.

That year, Big Sandy High School set a national record by scoring 824 points, a record that stood until 1994. However, more amazing than the offense was the defense, which only allowed 15 points all season, including eleven shutouts.

"The thing about the 15 points is that on the two touchdowns we gave up, the defensive back fell down," chuckled Smith, who led the Chicago Bears, as the team's head coach, to Super Bowl XLI against the Indianapolis Colts in 2007. "To this day, when I see my former teammates, you will always hear one of them say, 'Hey, you remember when?' I'm like, 'Shoot, do I remember when? Yeah, the memories are still very vivid.'"

Lovie Lee Smith was born on May 8, 1958, in Gladewater, Texas, but was raised in Big Sandy. Big Sandy didn't have any industry in town; it was a dairy and farming town with the farm crops being sweet potatoes and watermelons.

Smith said that like in any small town during that time, he played whatever sport was in season. He said that all the kids in town were close since they grew up playing sports against each other. Big Sandy didn't have a Pop Warner program, so it wasn't until the seventh grade that the neighborhood got to play competitively against someone else outside of town.

"In grade school, we were all playing whatever sport we could play. There was only one team in town and all the kids played on that team, no matter what the sport," said Smith. "And then there were the [Dallas] Cowboys. Church and then the Cowboys on Sunday.

"I was a huge Roger Staubach fan...he was my hero," recalled Smith. "Fortunately, in my life, I've had the chance to meet a lot of people, but I'd never met Roger. After going to the Super

Bowl, I was the Grand Marshall of a NASCAR race outside of Chicago. My family was there, and two of my sons spotted Roger and said 'Dad, Roger Staubach is here.' So I went to a tent where he was, and I introduced myself to him. He said 'I know who you are.' Wow, talk about standing up a little taller and putting your chest out a little bigger. You know, we all want the people we idolize to be a certain way, and Roger lived up to that. Man, it made my day!"

How small was Big Sandy in the '70s? The senior graduating class totaled thirty-four students.

"We were all very close," reminisced Smith. "We had each other's back. The thing that most people who haven't played on a team don't know is how close you become. Teammates become just like brothers. It's a bond that you have forever. I feel that way about my teammates' kids, their grandkids. It becomes a big, extended family."

And that family extended to the residents of the community that would turn out in force to watch their Wildcats roll to victory after victory. From 1971 through 1975, Big Sandy was 61–1–1.

"That Friday Night Lights thing that we now all know about was definitely Big Sandy," said Smith, who played on both sides of the ball but was the heart of the defense from his linebacker position. "When you're in a small town like Big Sandy, everyone went to the game. Just like everything revolved around church on Sundays, everything revolved around football on Fridays.

"Everyone knew something special was happening at that time," Smith added. "The beautiful thing about those years is that it didn't matter if you were black or white. Remember, it was the '70s, but half of my friends were white and half were black.

It didn't matter. Sports, in general, has done so much to advance the quality of life and getting along and respecting your fellow guy based on what he has done."

Smith was lucky enough to play on all three of Big Sandy's championship teams. In 1973, Big Sandy won the Class B championship by beating Rule, 25–0. The 1974 team was actually declared co-champs after battling Celina, led by legendary head coach G. A. Moore, to a 0–0 tie in the championship game. While every championship was sweet, Smith said nothing beat that 1975 season.

With most of the starters playing less than half of the games, the Wildcats rolled to lopsided victories during the regular season, including a 91–0 shellacking of Carlisle. Other scores from that season were 73–0 (Harmony), 71–0 (Mount Enterprise), 66–0 (Union Grove), 63–0 (Como-Pickton), 62–0 (Leverett's Chapel), 60–0 (Union Hill), 54–0 (Sabine), and 43–0 (Winona). The only regular season points the Wildcats allowed were in a 55–7 win over Hawkins.

"What people should know is that Coach [Jim] Norman kept the score down," said Smith. "I remember one game, David Overstreet touched the ball six times and scored six touchdowns and then didn't play in the second half. Quite honestly, that national scoring record could have been so far out of reach if coach hadn't held back. If he didn't hold back, you'd be talking about Big Sandy's total points to this day."

Aledo High School in Texas currently holds the national scoring record with 1,023 points scored during the 2013 season. Big Sandy is still ninth on the all-time list.

Big Sandy's head coach Jim Norman, who also served as the town's mayor, is someone whom Smith, no pun intended, loved. Lovie said that his head coach believed in everyone learning a second position and keeping things simple. "When Coach Norman came, things just changed. It wasn't like we were inventing football, but some of the things that he taught us are still with me today as a coach. He convinced us that we were going to play harder than everybody. He wanted us to give maximum effort throughout. He always wanted us to be competing. In order to play football in the fall, we had to run track in the spring."

While everyone in 1975 was watching Big Sandy's scoreboard like it was a pinball machine, the defense just kept putting up goose eggs, with nine shutouts in ten regular season games.

"During that time, that's what was expected of us…do your best and trust your teammates," recalled Smith. "It was a simple philosophy that paid off."

Big Sandy faced Groom in the Class B state championship game in '75 with eleven shutouts in thirteen games. With David Overstreet and the Wildcat defense capturing most of the headlines, a couple of other Big Sandy players had outstanding seasons. Quarterback Gary Chalk entered the championship game with 850 yards rushing while averaging over 14 yards per carry. Tony Newman, who played alongside Overstreet, had 1,375 yards with 27 touchdowns. Newman averaged 12.5 yards per carry while Overstreet brought a 23.4 yards per carry average into the title game.

As far as the numbers were concerned, Coach Norman was quoted in most newspapers as saying it was no big deal.

The Wildcat defense was its stout self in a 28–2 victory in the state championship game. Big Sandy fell on three fumbles and picked off two passes in the victory.

The most surprising thing about the victory was that Big Sandy actually trailed 2–0 after one quarter. Groom's Art Brown tackled Overstreet in the end zone midway through the quarter. Smith recovered a fumble late in the first quarter that led to Big Sandy's first score early in the second quarter, and the Fighting Wildcats never looked back.

The 1975 Big Sandy team was so dominant that five players were named to the Texas Sports Writers Association's All-State first team. Smith joined Newman on the defensive unit, with Overstreet and Chalk being joined on the first team offense by guard Frank Davis. Eleven players from that team made the Coaches All-District 9-B team, with Smith being named the district's Outstanding Defensive Player. Joining Smith on the first team defense were defensive linemen Larry Cuba and Mike Gibson, along with Newman at defensive back. Overstreet, who was the district's Outstanding Offensive Player, was also a first-team linebacker.

"That 1975 championship feeling was special," said Smith. "Whenever anybody calls to talk about Big Sandy, I'll always take time out of my schedule to talk about the town, the team, the coaches, and the players."

AFTER HIGH SCHOOL

Smith attended the University of Tulsa, where he was a two-time All-American. He began his coaching career immediately after graduating from Tulsa, returning to Big Sandy High School to serve as the team's defensive coordinator. One year later, he took a job at Cascia Hall Preparatory School in Tulsa. He stayed there two years before heading to the college ranks at his alma mater. He began his professional coaching career in 1996 as an assistant for the Tampa Bay Buccaneers. He became the head coach of the Chicago Bears in 2004 and remained in that position until 2012. Smith is currently the head coach at the University of Illinois.

16

LaDainian Tomlinson—University High School—Waco, Texas

WHEN YOU THINK of LaDainian Tomlinson, you think of thousands of yards rushing. But what you probably don't know is that at Waco's University High School, Tomlinson really enjoyed delivering blows as an outside linebacker.

"I really enjoyed stopping offenses," said Tomlinson. "From the linebacker position, I was able to use my speed by lining up on the edge and getting to the quarterback. Honestly, I had the mentality that there was no tackle that was going to be able to stop me because of my speed."

LaDainian Tramayne Tomlinson was born on June 23, 1979, in Rosebud, Texas, a tiny town of about 1,400 residents south of Waco. He recalled that the first time he did anything competitive was when he was five or six years old and he entered in the NFL's Punt, Pass, and Kick competition, which he said he won. He then began playing Pop Warner football at eight years old in Waco. The first time Tomlinson ever touched the ball in a game, he scored a touchdown.

"I was the quarterback on my Pop Warner team," Tomlinson said. "I always thought that quarterbacks called their own plays. So my coach comes up to me before my first game to tell me what we were going to run the first time we had the ball. He said, 'I want you to take the ball and roll out to the right and then just run with it.' I said, 'No, I want to give it to my friend Steven.' He said, 'No, I don't want you to give it to Steven. I'm calling the plays, not you, and I want you to run it.' I said, 'OK, Coach.'

"So on that first play, I did what Coach said, and I scored a touchdown. But here's the funny part: the play was called back because of a penalty. Then Coach told me to run the same exact play but to roll out to the left instead of the right. It worked, and I scored a touchdown on that run."

How much did he love the game? He actually slept with a football as a youngster.

"I guess I started sleeping with a football around junior high school," recalled Tomlinson. "My dream was to always play in the National Football League, so I tried to do everything I could [including sleeping with a football] to envision what it would take to be a professional football player."

Tomlinson, who really didn't have a relationship with his father, said that he looked up to his older cousin Broderick Lowe, who played wide receiver. When LT was inducted into the Pro Football Hall of Fame in 2017, he acknowledged Lowe during his induction speech saying, "Broderick, not only were you my inspiration but a father figure throughout my life."

Outside of the family, Tomlinson said that he looked up to Dallas Cowboys' running back Emmitt Smith. LaDainian said that he could relate to Smith when it came to size and determination. During his Hall of Fame induction ceremony, he recounted a special meeting with his idol when he was twelve years old, thanks to his mother working hard to help LT with his dream.

"It was my mom's sacrifice that led me to my first meeting with one of my football idols," said Tomlinson to the crowd in Canton on August 5, 2017. "When I was twelve and seriously lacking any self-confidence as an athlete, I spotted a flyer at the Boys and Girls Club. It had Emmitt Smith's picture on it. I thought it was Emmitt's football camp; actually it was the great Cowboys tight end Jay Novacek's camp and Emmitt and other great Cowboys were scheduled to attend.

"I rushed home and said, 'Mom, Emmitt Smith is having a football camp, I have to go.' She looked at the flyer and replied, 'That's too much money, baby. I don't know if we can make that happen.' A couple of months later mom called me into the room and said, 'Remember that Jay Novacek camp you wanted to go to?' I said, 'Yes ma'am.' She continued, 'Well, I saved

119

the money and you'll be able to go.' Wow. That's where I first saw Michel Irving, Emmitt, Jay, Darrell Johnson, and other Cowboys greats.

"I vividly remember the first practice. We were learning a hand-off drill, and I lined up with all the other running backs. Emmitt suddenly jumps in the line and hands the ball off to me. Then later that evening I was heading upstairs to dinner when Emmitt was coming downstairs and literally ran me over. I began to fall, but he held me up and asked, 'Are you alright kid?' I answered, 'Yeah I'm fine,' but the truth was I wasn't. I was awestruck because of two astonishing moments with my idol, a twelve-year-old kid lacking self-confidence as an athlete, left on top of the world feeling he could truly fulfill his dream to play in the National Football League."

LaDainian said that he learned about sacrifice from his mom. "I knew how hard she worked for me. Not only to get me into that camp but in many other ways. I was always grateful. She was working two jobs because that's what she needed to do to provide and, as a kid, I understood exactly what she was doing.

"There were times when if we didn't have it, we didn't have it. I remember one Christmas we didn't have one present under the tree. The tree was up, the lights were on, but not one present. I remember my mom and stepdad telling me, my brother, and sister that it was going to be Christmas without gifts. We thought it was a joke, but it wasn't. And when you go through things like that, you become very appreciative of the sacrifices that my mom made for all of us."

After moving from Waco back to Marlin, LT's high school career began at Marlin High School where he played on varsity as a freshman. He said that's where he began believing that he had a special talent.

"When I first started working out at Marlin in the summer, I heard whispers about me playing varsity, but I didn't want to play varsity," remembered Tomlinson. "I wanted to play with my peers on the freshman team. I remember that the head coach called me into his office and said, 'Son, I'm going to play you on the varsity.' I told him that I didn't want to play varsity and that's when he told me that I was 'too good' to play with the freshmen. I really didn't believe what coach was telling me.

"So he decided that he'd let me practice with both teams. Then one day during fall camp he made me a believer in myself. He had me go one-on-one in a tackling drill against a senior line-backer. Coach said, 'Down, set, hut.' I just took off and ran the linebacker over. The guys on the team went crazy. Coach came over to me and said, 'I told you son, you can play on this level [varsity].' Coach really did boost my confidence with that drill."

Tomlinson said he didn't get a lot of playing time on the varsity because of a senior running back who got most of the carries. He said he was used as a kickoff and punt returner for his first four varsity games. That's when he asked his coach to send him down to the freshman team to keep sharp.

"Coach agreed to send me down, and that's when I went nuts," said Tomlinson. "I was just running for a lot of yards. Prior to me coming down, the freshman team hadn't won a game, but while I was there, we didn't lose a game. After those three or four games, Coach moved me back to varsity."

Before the start of his sophomore season, his family moved to Waco where he played linebacker and fullback for University High School.

"The first thing I did was visit my new school to meet the head football coach LeRoy Coleman," Tomlinson said. "I thought I was the best thing since sliced bread. So when he asked me, 'What position do you play?' I answered proudly with my chest puffed out, 'I play running back and outside linebacker.' He looked at me and replied, 'No you don't. We have enough running backs, you're going to play fullback.' That was an important lesson to be selfless. I played fullback and outside linebacker for the next two years."

Tomlinson said that Coach Coleman made him understand what it meant to be a selfless player who sacrificed for the team by waiting his turn. The waiting paid off for LT and his teammates. Finally getting his chance to play tailback during his senior season in 1996, the University Trojans put together a great season.

After scoring only four touchdowns in ten games during his junior year, LT ran for six touchdowns in his first game as a starting tailback, rushing for 181 yards on 15 carries. From that moment on the entire state of Texas knew that Tomlinson was a force to be reckoned with.

With LT driving defenses crazy, University High made its deepest run ever into the state playoffs. The Trojans advanced to the state quarterfinals in Class 4A Division II, where they lost to Calallen. Tomlinson finished the season with 39 touchdowns.

"Me and my teammates took the University Trojans as far as they had ever gone," Tomlinson said. "We were two games away from state. That was a special, special team that still goes down as the best team in school history."

Tomlinson closed out his high school career playing for the South All-Stars in the annual Texas High School Coaches Association's North/South All-Star Game in Fort Worth. Tomlinson was on the same team as his future San Diego Chargers teammate Drew Brees. Tomlinson and Brees led the South to a 40–13 victory. Tomlinson carried the ball ten times for 27 yards, plus he caught two passes in the game before heading to TCU.

"Back then, Drew and I became good friends," said Tomlinson. "It was just one of those things where we just hit it off. The one thing that I remember about that game is that I caught a diving pass from him [Brees]. He was rolling out to the right, running for his life, and I came streaking across the field, and he threw on the run, and I dove and caught it.

"I remember during college that we'd go to these college award banquets and we'd talk about how funny it would be if we ended up on the same pro team. And, by golly, we did."

The interesting thing about the Tomlinson-Brees connection is that LT retired after his 2011 season after playing with the New York Jets, and Brees is still throwing passes on his way to the Pro Football Hall of Fame.

"I knew that he was special," said Tomlinson. "He's going to play until he's fifty…or at least he's going to try."

AFTER HIGH SCHOOL

Tomlinson accepted a scholarship to TCU, where he played for four years. After splitting time with another running back during his freshman and sophomore seasons, Tomlinson became the Horned Frogs' No. 1 back as a junior. He had an incredible junior year in 1999 with 1,974 yards rushing, which was the most in the NCAA that season. Tomlinson also broke the single-game rushing record with 406 yards against UTEP. That record stood until 2014.

Tomlinson's senior season was even better, as he led the nation in rushing for the second straight year with 2,158 yards with 22 touchdowns. He was named an All-American for that performance. His 5,387 career yards places him 12th on the NCAA's all-time career yards list.

The San Diego Chargers selected Tomlinson with the fifth overall pick in the 2001 NFL Draft. When he retired after the 2011 season, he was fifth on the NFL's all-time rushing yards list with 13,684. Tomlinson was elected to the College Football Hall of Fame in 2014 and the Pro Football Hall of Fame in 2017, which was his first year of eligibility.

17

Elmo Wright—Sweeny High School— Sweeny, Texas

IF YOU'RE A fan of end zone celebrations, then you should be a fan of Elmo Wright. While at the University of Houston, Wright became the first football player to ever do an end zone dance. The All-American receiver was known to high-step into the end zone at the end of long touchdown receptions.

Elmo Wright was born on July 3, 1949, in Brazoria, Texas, a small town of about 3,000 residents around 60 miles south of Houston. Like so many others we've mentioned thus far, Wright did not play football until high school. Instead, he was a member of the school band from third through tenth grade. The only reason he tried out for the football team as a junior was because the band director had belittled him for getting his lip busted playing around with a football.

"I was in the band from the third through the tenth grade," said Wright. "I went to watch all of the football games, and my older brother L. C. played on the football team at Carver, but I played the tenor saxophone. I was a musician.

"So one day I'm walking by a PE [physical education] class and some guy yelled, 'Hey Elmo!' I turned my head and *WHAM*, a football hits me right in the mouth and splits my lip. I'm telling you that he could throw the ball a thousand times and he wouldn't have been able to do that again. Anyway, my band coach didn't have a sense of humor about the whole deal. He really got on me, and I just had enough, so I just quit the band right then and there."

So with no band to play with, Wright decided to play football. Even though he had watched a lot of games, he still wasn't really sure about how things would turn out, as he had never attended a PE class.

"I can remember the first time I was in a huddle," recalled Wright. "The quarterback called the play and then looked at me and said, 'Elmo, run five yards and stop.' I said, 'OK.' Then, instead of running like you would normally see someone run on a football field, I kind of limped out for five yards and turned around. Man, that quarterback whistled one at me that hit me so hard that it just stuck in my stomach.

"So then I turn around and one of my favorite words is 'run' and that's what I did...I was running for my life. That's really how I developed my style of running. I was elusive. I was pretty fast, and I had a lot of fear. It was 100 percent fear when it came to football, but I guess it helped that I sort of knew a little bit of what to do because of watching all those games."

Despite his late start, Wright had the unique distinction of playing on two state championship teams—one pre-segregation and one post-segregation—in Sweeny, Texas. In 1965, He and his teammates at Carver High School won a Prairie View Interscholastic League Class 1A title, which was the PVIL's smallest classification. Then in 1966, after Carver was integrated with Sweeny High School, Wright played on Sweeny's Class 2A University Interscholastic League state championship team.

In 1965, Wright was part of the Carver High team that was considered one of the strongest in the PVIL. Heading into the state semifinals against Willis High School, Wright, who played both ways for the Wildcats, had caught 21 passes for 407 yards and seven touchdowns. After battling to a 0–0 draw at the half, Carver beat Willis 22–6. He intercepted a pass in the second half that led to one of the Wildcats' three touchdowns. The win moved Carver into the state championship game against Cameron Price.

Carver beat Cameron Price, 21–14, for the 1A state title. The win gave Carver a 10–2 record in the school's final year of existence. The Wildcats outscored their opponents 296–82.

At the end of his junior season, Wright, who was vice president of Carver High's Student Council, was named All-State and his coach Elijah Childers termed Wright as the key man in the team's championship run.

"It was kind of funny that I was named All-State since I had only been playing football for four months. I thought to myself that All-State must not be a big deal if I could be named All-State with so little football experience," laughed Wright.

The addition of Wright and two of his other All-State teammates from Carver was expected to help Sweeny High, which was 4–4–2 in 1965. Wright said that the integration of the two teams went very smoothly.

"You have to remember that Sweeny really had two different sides of town back then," stated Wright. "You had the black side and the white side. Really, if you turned left, you were in the black community, and if you turned right, you were in the white community.

"In many ways, the integration was sad, because all of the black culture went away. The school went away. The stadium was torn down, but the Sweeny coaches knew how to help us cross over. They understood synergy, and that made the transition easier. Remember, you can bring things together and make things better or you can bring things together and make things worse. I don't know how the coaches knew how to do what they did, but Sweeny became better as a result."

Wright said that all of the coaches were great at Sweeny, especially Ken Dabbs, who was the team's offensive coordinator. Yes, the same Coach Dabbs who is the sole reason that Earl Campbell became a Texas Longhorn. As you've probably figured out by now, Coach Dabbs's fingerprints are all over Texas high school and college football.

Dabbs, who also served as Sweeny High's head track coach, knew a thing or two about talent—especially a talent that could run like Elmo could run.

"Elmo Wright was the best receiver I had ever seen," said Dabbs. "He could run the 40 in 4.5 seconds. He weighed about 180 pounds and was smart in the classroom. I spent a lot of time with him because I would drive him home after football practices because there were no school buses running at that time. Elmo holds a very special spot in my heart."

Sweeny's 1966 offense was high-powered, with Elmo Wright leading the way alongside quarterback Jim Lindsey, who would become a top professional quarterback in the Canadian Football League. The Bulldogs were ranked the No. 1 team in the state in Class 2A. That ranking was helped by a great start that saw Sweeny get out to a 3–0 record with all their wins coming against larger 3A schools. The Bulldogs outscored their first three opponents by a total of 104–0.

After a perfect regular season, the Bulldogs headed into the postseason. Sweeny opened the playoffs with a 6–0 win over Edna. The Wildcats then shutout Kenedy 43–0 to win the regional championship. Wright caught one touchdown pass in the Kenedy victory.

After a 21–14 defeat of San Antonio Randolph in the state quarterfinals, Wright and his teammates were set for a semifinal match-up against Bastrop. Elmo was great on both sides of the ball. Wright caught touchdown passes of 15 and 12 yards in a 15–7 victory. On defense, he had three interceptions to send his team to the state Class 2A State Championship against Granbury.

Both teams entered the state championship game in Austin undefeated with high-powered offenses. Granbury had scored 486 points while Sweeny had posted 438. After trailing 7–6 at the half, Sweeny scored three touchdowns in the second half and relied on its strong defense to capture state gold with a 29–7 victory. Sweeny, which finished with a perfect 14–0 record, didn't complete a pass in the state championship game, but Wright did catch a two-point conversion to give Sweeny a 14–7 lead, plus returned a punt for a score. He was also an important part of the strong Bulldog defense that shutout Granbury in the second half.

"We knew they [Granbury] were going to double-team him [Wright], so we decided to abandon our passing game and run right at them," said Dabbs. "They had us 7–0 with about a minute until halftime. They punted, and Elmo returned it 75 yards or so for a touchdown. In the second half, we ran the ball right at them, and they couldn't stop us."

For his outstanding senior season, Wright was named to the Texas Sports Writers Association's Class 2A All-State Team. Wright's quarterback Jim Lindsey was named to the second team.

While many got to know Wright as the guy that did football's first end zone dance, it shouldn't detract from the fact that he was an extremely talented football player.

"At that time as an athlete, you could put him up against anybody," said Dabbs. "Elmo could do it all. He was a diamond in the rough and one of the best ever, even as a defensive back. You have to remember that Elmo was voted the '60s Athlete of the Decade in Texas. That really tells you how good Elmo Wright was."

AFTER HIGH SCHOOL

After graduating from Sweeny, Wright attended the University of Houston. It was with the Cougars where the man that liked to run began the practice of "high-stepping" on his long touchdown catch and carries.

During his sophomore season in 1968, Wright would spike the ball after scoring his touchdowns. The spike had become a popular way of celebrating scores in 1965 when Homer Jones of the New York Giants started it. However, heading into the 1969 season, the NCAA outlawed the spike.

With the spike gone from his celebrations, Wright explained how the dance began on September 20, 1969, when Houston played the University of Florida in Gainesville. "I ran a down-and-out pattern and caught the ball. The cornerback dove at my feet, which caused me to high-step to get away from the tackle. Since there were no other players in front of me, I continued to high-step into the end zone. I was very excited!

"I can remember people booing me, but I high-stepped all the way to the sidelines. You have to remember that segregation was still the norm, so people were getting so mad. But my teammates loved it when I got to the sidelines. Bottom line, it felt so good that I decided to keep doing it. Football should be fun!"

Wright became an All-American receiver for Houston. He led the nation in touchdown receptions in 1969, and in 1970, he was an All-American. He left the school as its all-time leader in receiving yards with 3,347 and 34 touchdowns. He's still fourth on the all-time list for receiving yards and second on the all-time TD list.

The Kansas City Chiefs selected Wright with the 16th overall pick in the first round of the 1971 NFL Draft. He high-stepped his way to six NFL touchdowns.

18

Texas Heisman Trophy Winners

THE HEISMAN TROPHY was first presented in 1935. That year, the award was officially called the Downtown Athletic Club (DAC) Trophy, which was awarded to the Outstanding College Football Player East of the Mississippi River.

Jay Berwanger, a halfback at the University of Chicago, was the first recipient, followed by two winners from Yale—end Larry Kelley in 1936 and halfback Clint Frank in 1937.

In 1938, the name of the award was changed to the Heisman Trophy to honor of the DAC's athletic director John Heisman, who died in 1936. With the name change, the boundaries for the award were widened to include the entire country. The winner that year was Davey O'Brien of TCU, who became the first of ten Texans to win the prestigious award. In December 2017, Oklahoma quarterback Baker Mayfield, who played his high school football at Lake Travis High School in Austin, became the tenth Texan to win the Heisman.

Heisman Trophy Winners from Texas High School Football

2017: Baker Mayfield, Lake Travis
2012: Johnny Manziel, Kerrville Tivy
2011: Robert Griffin III, Copperas Cove
1990: Ty Detmer, San Antonio Southwest
1989: Andre Ware, Dickinson
1987: Tim Brown, Woodrow Wilson
1978: Billy Sims, Hooks
1977: Earl Campbell, John Tyler
1948: Doak Walker, Highland Park
1938: Davey O'Brien, Woodrow Wilson

TIM BROWN—WOODROW WILSON HIGH SCHOOL— DALLAS, TEXAS

Up until 2004, Dallas' Woodrow Wilson High School was the only high school in America that could claim two winners. Wilson alum and Texas Christian University quarterback Davey O'Brien, who now has his own award honoring the nation's top

QB every year, won the award in 1938. In 1987, Wilson wide receiver Tim Brown won his Heisman while playing for Notre Dame.

For those of you wondering, the other school with two winners is Mater Dei High School in Santa Ana, California. (Former Monarch John Huarte, a quarterback at Notre Dame, won the award in 1964, while University of South California quarterback Matt Leinart was the winner in 2001.)

Timothy Donnell Brown was born on July 22, 1996, in Dallas to parents Eugene and Josephine Brown, who grew up in Louisiana but moved to Dallas in the early '60s. To say Tim was destined for football fame and Canton at an early age wouldn't be accurate. Even if Brown was blessed with God-given football skills, his mother Josephine was not a fan of the game and forbade him from playing. The use of the phrase God-given is an accurate way to describe why Josephine didn't want her son on the gridiron.

Josephine was the daughter of a Baptist preacher whose Pentecostal beliefs were that sports were "the Antichrist" in Tim's words through various media reports. According to his mom's bible teachings, a man can't serve two Gods. Josephine, along with other church members, believed that sports had the potential to become someone's God, therefore putting God second.

What is unusual is there was plenty of athletic talent in the Brown family. His older brother Wayne is said to have been an outstanding running back in high school, while his sister Gwen was an All-District volleyball player and his sister Ann was All-District in track who went on to be an All-American volleyball player in college.

In his Pro Football Hall of Fame induction speech, Brown talked about learning to play the game of football on the playgrounds of Mount Auburn Elementary School and on Culver Street in Dallas.

"Imagine this, there is a concrete street and there are two sides and on each side there was a patch of grass," said Brown. "We used to call it 'throw up football.' You throw the ball up…whoever gets it…you get to run. Well, if you got on the sideline though, you got tackled. So thinking that you can grab a ball and run down the sideline and tackle the guy and land on the grass was not the smartest thing in the world, and it is the reason why I have all of these scars and all this happened way before I got into playing real football. But it's the reason I learned how to juke and dodge guys and stay away from the sidelines."

Tim played football in the seventh grade but eventually stopped playing the game. During his freshman year at Wilson, Brown was actually in the school's marching band, where he played the bass drum.

"I was a percussionist, but I could only play the bass drum, because the older guys weren't going to carry the big bass drum… they were making the freshmen carry the big bass drum," Brown said. "I think if I would have gotten the chance to play the percussions, I would have really loved band."

In addition to enjoying music at that time, Brown also enjoyed basketball. He had more dreams of playing hoops at Duke or North Carolina than playing football at Notre Dame. Brown was also a standout on the Wilson track team in the 400-meter dash and long jump.

When the man known as Mr. Raider, because of his incredible NFL career with the Los Angeles/Oakland Raiders, began playing football at the Dallas Independent School District high school, he kept it a secret from his mother. To explain why he was going to football games every Friday night, he told an unsuspecting Josephine that he was playing bass drum in the marching band.

When he made the varsity team as a sophomore, he had to give up his music career and get a parents' signature on some forms before he could hit the field. His father signed his football papers without telling his mom. His mother never saw Tim play football in person during his time at Wilson, but she really wasn't missing much.

The truth of the matter was that Woodrow Wilson wasn't very good during Brown's three years on the team. In fact, two wins a season was the most Tim and his teammates would celebrate from 1981 to 1983. The Wildcats record during that stretch was 4–25–1, a fact that Brown pointed out during his Hall of Fame speech in Canton.

However, there was one game out of those thirty that changed Brown's life forever. It came against Wilson's arch-rival, Skyline, during his junior year.

"The University of Notre Dame came to recruit one of Skyline's players," said Brown. "They didn't know anything about me. On that particular night, I had a kickoff return for a touchdown. I had a punt return for a touchdown. I had a long pass for a touchdown, and I had a long run for a touchdown. Now that was a great night. Now, if Notre Dame would have come the week before, I scored one touchdown. If they would have come the week afterward, I didn't score at all."

And, with that, Tim Brown became a highly recruited high school football prospect who chose the University of Notre Dame where he won the Heisman Trophy in 1987 during which time his mother, who still hadn't seen him play in person, said that she still hoped that Tim would become a minister.

After High School

At Notre Dame, Brown became known as "Touchdown Timmy." He was a two-time All-American who left South Bend with nineteen different school records. In 2009, Brown, who was the first receiver to win the Heisman, was inducted into the College Football Hall of Fame.

Brown's NFL career began when the Los Angeles Raiders selected him with the sixth overall pick in the 1988 NFL Draft. Brown retired with 14,934 yards receiving, the second-highest total in NFL history. He caught 1,094 catches with 100 touchdowns to go along with 19,682 total yards of offense. In 2015, Brown was inducted into the Pro Football Hall of Fame

BAKER MAYFIELD—LAKE TRAVIS HIGH SCHOOL— AUSTIN, TEXAS

Baker Reagan Mayfield was born on April 14, 1995. His dad was a backup quarterback at the University of Houston.

As a junior quarterback, Baker Mayfield stepped into the middle of one of Texas' greatest championship runs. Mayfield took over the offensive reigns of the Lake Travis Cavaliers in 2011, leading the school to its fifth-straight state championship. The

2017 Heisman Trophy winner said that LT's winning tradition had deep roots by the time he arrived on the scene.

"In 2007, we lost to Westlake," said Mayfield, who hadn't arrived on the high school campus yet but enjoys talking about the Cavs' success. "After that, we won 48 straight. Lake Travis standards when I was growing up were very high."

After the 28–21 loss to arch-rival Westlake, Lake Travis went 1,099 days without a loss. Fellow Texas high school football powerhouse Aledo snapped LT's 48-game win streak on September 10, 2010. The Cavs would lose one more regular season game in 2010, but the season ended with the Cavs hoisting their fourth-straight state title that set the stage for Baker's two-year run as the team's starting quarterback.

The QB position at Lake Travis became high profile, starting with current NFL quarterback Garrett Gilbert who led Lake Travis to state titles in 2007 and 2008. Michael Brewer, who went on to a college career at Texas Tech and Virginia Tech, quarterbacked the school to its next two titles.

When Mayfield entered high school, he wasn't exactly looking like Heisman Trophy or NFL material. He was 5-foot-3 and weighed 150 pounds. In 2009, Mayfield was a quarterback on Lake Travis' freshman team. He was the JV quarterback in 2010.

"There was a lot of hard work with great coaches," said Mayfield. "Growing up there instilled a work ethic. It taught me to go for it and burn it."

In the spring of 2011, Mayfield finished second in a four-player battle for the starting position. However, Mayfield's title of backup QB was dropped on the very first drive of the regular season against Westlake when starting quarterback Colin Lagasse was tackled on a long run that separated his shoulder. In came Mayfield, and the rest is history.

In that game, Mayfield beat Westlake, the same team that in 2007 was the springboard to the 48-game win streak, by passing for nearly 300 yards and one touchdown, in addition to running for 94 yards and two scores in a 35–7 victory. Over the next two games, Mayfield took it to the next level with six touchdown passes against Aledo and five against Hendrickson. The Aledo game saw him complete 27-of-37 passes for 468 yards.

Even after Lagasse became healthy, Mayfield stayed the starter. Lagasse was moved to running back where he became the team's second-leading rusher. Baker and the Cavs never looked back during the regular season in 2011. Aside from the season-ending 24–21 win over Cedar Park in the regular-season finale, LT beat its opponents by an average of 36 points.

Not much changed in the playoffs with big victories over McCallum (58–7), Smithson Valley (42–21), and Flour Bluff (58–15) in the first three rounds of the Class 4A Division I play-offs. Mayfield tossed nine touchdowns in those three games and ran for two more. In the quarterfinals, Lake Travis had a rematch against District 25-4A foe, Cedar Park, who they beat four weeks earlier by three points for the district championship. The Cavs came away with a 14–9 win to advance to the state semis where they cruised past Dawson, 45–14, behind four Mayfield TD passes.

In the state championship game at AT&T Stadium, home of the Dallas Cowboys, Mayfield and Lake Travis became the first team in Texas high school football history to win five straight state football titles with a 22–7 win over Midway. The game was played before more than 33,000 fans.

Ironically, it was Mayfield and Lagasse who played the biggest roles on offense. Mayfield was 24-of-39 for 276 yards with a touchdown, while Lagasse was the game's Offensive Most Valuable Player with 210 yards of total offense and a touchdown.

"My junior year favorite memory is hard to say because there's nothing better than 16–0 and a state championship at Cowboys Stadium," said Mayfield.

Mayfield closed out the year having completed 247-of-378 yards (65.3 percent) for 3,788 yards with 45 touchdowns and only five interceptions. He also ran for 754 yards and 10 touchdowns.

Unfortunately, the 2012 season didn't turn out the way Mayfield and his teammates had hoped, as the Cavs finished the regular season 9–1. The drive for six straight state titles started with Lake Travis on a state-record 30 game playoff win streak against Pflugerville, which brought a 7–3 record into the game.

Mayfield's 60-yard run, the first of two rushing touchdowns for Baker, gave the Cavs a 7–6 halftime lead. LT took a 20–16 lead with just over three minutes to go in the game. But Pflugerville came right back and scored with 41 seconds remaining, giving the Panthers a 23–20 lead. In true Baker style, he launched a 51-yard Hail Mary pass with no time on the clock that was caught by Grant Foster. However, officials ruled that Foster was out of bounds, giving Pflugerville the 23–20 upset victory.

"Unfortunately, my senior year we snapped our playoff winning streak, but playing with those guys and seeing where they are now...it's been a fun process," said Mayfield. "We had a special group of coaches around us and a great community that supported us so we could have success.

"At Lake Travis, if you were a good player, you could start for two years. It was very rare to have someone start for three. It was very competitive. You had to earn your spot. Nothing was given because of the talent level and depth we had. It taught me how to work for it and how to earn it and to hate losing. I always hated losing. To rarely do it [lose] in high school helped me develop that mentality. I carried that to Norman [University of Oklahoma]. It was the same mentally there, so it was an easy transition."

Baker finished his high school career with a 25–2 record. He threw for 6,255 yards with 67 touchdowns and only eight interceptions.

"Baker is a great player," says Lake Travis head coach Hank Carter. "I'm very excited for Baker and his future. He distributes the football well…can run it when he needs to…comes from a great family. His dad played quarterback at the University of Houston. Baker's one of those kids that never has a bad day… always has a smile on his face."

After High School

Mayfield headed to Texas Tech as a walk-on, where he became the first true freshman walk-on to start for a Football Bowl Series (FBS) team. Ironically, he became the starter due to an injury to fellow Lake Travis alum Michael Brewer before the start of the 2013 season. In his first game, he threw for over 400 yards and four touchdowns. He battled injuries and eventually lost the starting job but finished with over 2,300 yards passing with 12 touchdowns and nine interceptions. He left Texas Tech after that season, transferring to Oklahoma.

Mayfield was a three-year starter for the Sooners. He led OU to the College Football Playoff semifinals in 2015 and 2017, finishing his career with 129 career touchdowns. He finished third in the 2016 Heisman Trophy voting and won the prestigious award in 2017.

JOHNNY MANZIEL—TIVY HIGH SCHOOL—KERRVILLE, TEXAS

Before he became "Johnny Football," Johnny Manziel was a three-year starter at Tivy High School in Kerrville, a town of 23,000 people about an hour northwest of San Antonio. Manziel became the first freshman to ever win the Heisman Trophy.

While many now know Manziel as one of the NFL's most infamous crash-and-burn victims because of his off-field issues, I knew Johnny when he was considered one of the greatest playmakers in the hallowed history of Texas high school football. I was part of the nominating committee at the National High School Coaches Association that named the 6-foot-1, 195-pounder as its National Senior Football Athlete of the Year.

Along with Trish Hoffman, I interviewed Manziel in June 2011 on the *NHSCA Sports Hour* radio show to talk about winning the award and his high school memories.

"I really enjoyed the deep runs me and my teammates made in back-to-back years to the state semifinals in 2009 and 2010," recalled Manziel when thinking about his favorite high school memories. "There's really nothing like it. The football team was a huge part of the community, and we wouldn't have been anything without the community."

Manziel's high school career began as a receiver. He didn't start as the Antlers' quarterback until the fourth game of his sophomore season, but that's when people started calling him "Johnny Football." During his career as a receiver, Manziel caught 30 passes for 582 yards and five touchdowns.

He split time at quarterback and receiver throughout his 2008 sophomore season, finishing with 1,109 yards passing, 835 yards rushing, and 408 yards receiving while having his hand in 28 touchdowns.

During the 2009 season, with Manziel as the full-time starter at quarterback, the Antlers advanced to the Class 4A Division II state semifinals where they lost to Brenham, 31–21. Tivy finished with a 9–5 record after a 0–2 start. Manziel completed 211-of-349 attempts (60 percent) for 2,782 yards with 19 touchdowns and only five interceptions. The dual-threat QB averaged over 6.5 yards per carry on the ground with 1,529 yards rushing and 33 touchdowns.

As a senior in 2010, Manziel, who originally gave a verbal commitment to the University of Oregon before deciding to play college football at Texas A&M, helped take Tivy into the second round of the Class 4A Division I playoffs where the Antlers lost to eventual state champion Lake Travis.

Tivy finished 10–2 in 2010 with Manziel having his best season in high school with 3,609 yards passing and 1,674 rushing. He threw for 45 touchdowns and ran for 30 more. Manziel took pride in the fact that during his senior year he threw only five interceptions against 45 touchdowns.

"Being a quarterback, you take it personally when you throw an interception," said Manziel. "Whenever you see the other team running the other way with the ball, you know you just gave one up and you learn from your mistakes. If you cut down on turnovers, you have a better chance of winning the football game.

"They [the coaches] just gave the quarterbacks a lot of freedom, a lot of leeway and let us run the show," added Manziel. "We tried to spread defenses out, and if they wanted to take away our run, we'd throw it 70 times a game."

Manziel did just that on September 3, 2009, against San Antonio Madison when he set a state record for pass attempts in a single game that still stands today. He completed 41-of-75 passes for 503 yards and four touchdowns with no interceptions in a come-from-behind 39–34 victory.

Johnny Football's final high school stats read: 7,500 yards passing with 75 touchdowns, and 4,038 yards rushing with 78 touchdowns.

When I called Manziel's high school coach Mark Smith in 2011 to inform him about the award to set up the radio interview, Smith described him as, "a very talented, nice kid."

After High School

After first giving his verbal commitment to the University of Oregon, Manziel changed his mind and accepted a scholarship to play at Texas A&M University. He really wanted to play for the University of Texas.

After redshirting during his freshman season in 2011, Manziel began cultivating the legend of "Johnny Football," who first captured the national spotlight when he broke Archie Manning's forty-three-year-old total offense record in a game when he put up 557 yards against Florida. Two weeks later, he broke his own record with 576 yards in total offense against Louisiana Tech. By the time Manziel and his teammates upset No. 1 Alabama in Tuscaloosa, Alabama, Johnny Football was a must-see event in college football. He became the first freshman to win the Heisman Trophy at the end of the 2012 season.

Manziel entered the 2014 NFL Draft, instead of playing his junior season. After being projected as a Top 5 pick, he fell to 22nd overall, taken by the Cleveland Browns. After two turbulent years with the Browns, with problems ranging from injuries to alcohol and drug abuse, the Browns released him.

In 2017, Manziel began a journey to return to pro football by trying to land a contract to play in the Canadian Football League. In early 2018, Manziel announced that he had been diagnosed with bipolar disorder and was taking medication.

ROBERT GRIFFIN III—COPPERAS COVE HIGH SCHOOL—COPPERAS COVE, TEXAS

Griffin's life began on another continent. He was born in Okinawa, Japan, where his parents, Robert Jr. and Jacqueline, were stationed in the Army. When they retired from military duty, they settled in Copperas Cove.

Robert Lee Griffin III was born on February 12, 1990. At Copperas Cove High School, Griffin played three sports—basketball, football, and track. Griffin said that growing up he looked up to Copperas Cove alum Charles Tillman, who was in the early part of his NFL career as a defensive back with the Chicago Bears.

"I was in junior high school and he was fresh into the league, doing a good job," said Griffin about Tillman, during a USAA military event. "A lot of kids like myself looked up to him back in Copperas Cove. He came back and we were playing basketball. I was real shy and didn't want to ask him for his autograph. He doesn't remember this, but I walked up to him asking for his autograph and he told me, 'Keep at it young buck, my friend is telling me that you've got a lot of success ahead.'"

Griffin, who is nine years younger than Tillman, added, "He kind of showed a lot of the young kids in Copperas Cove—the military brats—that you can make it, no matter what's going on, how many times you move, no matter what happens with your family in the military. He also showed that you gotta give back."

Long before he was RGIII, his high school coach Jack Welch said there was no doubt that Griffin was going to be special. He said he knew as far back as the third grade.

"Oh, we knew who Robert was right from the start. I remember his younger sister was my office aide and she'd always say, 'Hey coach, you need to look at my little brother.' And, I'd say we *know* about your little brother," laughed Welch.

"What was really neat was Robert used to always send notes to my brother Tracy, our offensive coordinator and quarterback coach, when he was in the seventh and eighth grade," added Welch. "Robert would always sign those notes 'Your future Bull-dawg Quarterback.'"

Welch said that even in the third grade, Griffin was going to AAU track meets and setting national records.

"I always get asked if what he [Griffin] was doing on the football field surprised me?" Welch said. "My answer was no…he's been under the gun since the third and fourth grades."

Griffin finished his high school career with 3,357 yards passing with 41 touchdowns and only nine interceptions. He also ran for 2,161 yards and 32 touchdowns in his two years as the school's starting quarterback.

I'd be remiss if I didn't mention Griffin's track exploits. He broke the state records in the 110-meter (13.55 seconds) and 300-meter hurdles (35.33), just missing the national high school record in the 300 hurdles by 1/100th of a second. As a junior, Griffin was named the Gatorade Texas Track and Field Athlete of the Year. He was named the 2007 *USA Today* All-USA track and field team.

After High School

Griffin graduated early from Copperas Cove to enroll at Baylor University where he could play football and compete in track at a high level, as the Bears had an outstanding track and field program. Griffin started 11 of 12 games as a true freshman, being named the Big 12's Freshman of the Year. He closed out his collegiate career winning the 2011 Heisman Trophy.

Griffin was drafted No. 2 overall by the Washington Redskins in the 2012 NFL Draft. Griffin won the 2012 NFL Offensive Rookie of the Year Award but injured his knee. After injuries and a couple of down seasons, Griffin was cut by the Redskins, signed by the Cleveland Browns, and then released. In April 2018, Griffin signed with the Baltimore Ravens.

THE OTHERS

As a five-sport athlete at Southwest High School in San Antonio, Ty Detmer could do it all. He earned letters in baseball, basketball, football, golf, and track.

Playing for his father Sonny, who was the Dragons' head coach, the younger Detmer threw for over 1,100 yards during his sophomore year in 1984. Things went to another level in 1985 with Ty throwing between 50 and 80 passes a game. Detmer completed 209-of-371 passes for a record 3,551 yards with 36 touchdowns as the Dragons finished 12–1, losing in the second round of the state's 4A playoffs. The Amarillo Chamber of Commerce named Detmer the state's top player.

Before his senior season in 1986, Detmer announced that he would attend Brigham Young University. While the Dragons didn't make the playoffs, Detmer closed out his scholastic career as an All-American who shattered the state's all-time career yardage mark with 8,005 yards passing. He was the first Texas quarterback to top 8,000 yards. For his career, Detmer completed 506-of-910 attempts, giving him the state record in both categories.

Detmer won the Heisman Trophy in 1990. He was the second straight Texan to win the coveted award after Andre Ware won it in 1989. Ware played at Dickinson High School in Dickinson, Texas, just outside of Houston. Surprisingly, Ware, who would go on to break numerous passing records while running the pass-happy spread offense at the University of Houston, threw the ball rarely in high school because Dickinson used a run-oriented offensive attack.

Ware became the first African American quarterback to win the Heisman Trophy. He did it in 1989 after throwing for 4,699 yards and 44 touchdowns while setting 26 NCAA records.

• • •

Over forty years earlier, Doak Walker was an all-around star and athlete for Highland Park High School in Dallas. Walker played five sports in high school—baseball, basketball, football, swimming, and track and field, but being on the gridiron was his favorite. When he was a young boy, Walker, who would go on to win the Heisman at SMU, wrote a school paper on SMU fullback Harry Shuford when he was instructed to write about a great man.

During the 1943 season, Walker was the Scotties second star as the junior running back teamed up with future NFL star quarterback Bobby Layne to lead Highland Park to the Class 2A state semifinals, where they lost to eventual big school state champ San Angelo, 21–20.

With Layne graduated, the 1944 season was another outstanding one for Highland Park, with Walker leading the Scotties to the state championship game against Port Arthur. The game was played between Christmas and New Year's. With nearly 13,000 fans looking on at the University of Texas' Memorial Stadium, Port Arthur's defense shut down Walker and the Scotties highpowered passing attack. Walker completed only 15-of-43 passes for 154 yards and a touchdown in the 20–7 loss. Newspaper reports from the game state that Walker was under constant pressure, ending the game with minus-11 yards rushing.

The Associated Press and United Press International both named Walker to their First-Team All-State squads in 1944.

Thirty-five quarterbacks have won the Heisman Trophy, the most of any position. TCU's Davey O'Brien was the first. As we mentioned previously in this chapter, for the longest time, Woodrow Wilson in Dallas was the only high school in America able to claim two Heisman Trophy winners, with Tim Brown being the other.

While there are not a lot of newspaper reports on O'Brien from his time at Wilson in the early '30s, we do know that he led the school to the state playoffs in 1932 in Class A, which was the state's largest classification at the time. Wilson lost in the first round to Fort Worth Masonic, 40–7. Fort Worth Masonic advanced to the state championship, where it lost to Corsicana on penetrations after battling to a 0–0 tie.

19

Offensive Players

IN THE MODERN-DAY pass-happy world of Texas high school football, Drew Brees, Andy Dalton, and Andrew Luck do not appear in the state's record book. Instead, you'll find non-household names like Hunter Lile of Booker High School, Nick Gerber of Levelland High, and Travis Quintanilla of Refugio High School.

To give you an idea of how far the passing game has come, Brees graduated with 5,461 career passing yards and 50 touchdowns. Lile, who graduated in 2014, is Texas' all-time leader in passing yards (14,408), completions (1,047), and attempts (1,677) while tossing 162 touchdowns, which is third on the all-time list.

You also won't find Earl Campbell, Eric Dickerson, Craig James, or LaDainian Tomlinson listed on the all-time rushing records. While Dez Bryant's average of 50 catches per season at Lufkin was great then, the current single-season record holder is Jason Bird of Lake Travis who caught 153 balls in 2007, which is more than 100 over Bryant.

Bottom line: there are hundreds of outstanding players who have left their mark on the sport of Texas high school football before making it to Sunday afternoons. In this chapter, we'll take a look at some of the other that shined under the bright Friday Night Lights.

THE QUARTERBACKS

Sammy Baugh—Sweetwater High School—Sweetwater, Texas

"Slingin' Sammy" Baugh was a man ahead of his time when it came to throwing the football. During an era when three yards and a cloud of dust was the main way of moving the football, Baugh perfected the forward pass after his high school career.

Samuel Adrian Baugh was born on March 17, 1914, on a farm outside of Temple, Texas. He moved with his family to Sweetwater when he was sixteen years old after playing running back during his sophomore season for Temple. He played three sports for the Mustangs—football, basketball, and baseball. Many believed that Baugh was best at baseball. In fact, because Sweetwater High didn't have a baseball team, Baugh played for the Abilene Oilers, a semi-pro baseball team.

Baugh, who was part of the first class inducted into the College Football Hall of Fame in 1951 and Pro Football Hall of Fame in 1963, led Sweetwater to the playoffs during his junior and senior years in 1931 and 1932 by driving opponents crazy with his running and throwing in his halfback run-pass option.

A story that has been told a lot is that in high school, Baugh would practice with an old tire strung from a tree branch. It is said that he would try to throw the ball on the run through the tire while it was swinging, which may have finally switched him from running back to quarterback during his career at Texas Christian University.

At Sweetwater High School, Baugh wore No. 21, which was retired in 2006, becoming the only jersey number to be retired by the school district.

Baugh's senior season in 1932 was a great one for the Mustangs, who advanced to the state quarterfinals where they faced Amarillo High School. It was a snow-covered field that greeted Baugh and his boys that day in December at Butler Field.

Coming into the game, newspaper reports called Sweetwater's aerial attack one of the smoothest since the days of Boyce Magness of Breckenridge High School. Boyce "Boone" Mangess, a member of the Texas Sports Hall of Fame and Texas High School Football Hall of Fame, was considered the state's best dual-threat player, leading the Buckaroos from 1927–1929. Baugh's scholastic career came to a close with a 7[en dash]0 defeat before about 5,000 fans.

One interesting fact about Baugh that had nothing to do with football was that he fought in a boxing match on August 10, 1933. Slingin' Sammy became Swingin' Sammy when he took on Red Tolar in a boxing match in Abilene, Texas. The three-round fight was on the undercard of an event that included former heavyweight champ Jack Dempsey as the referee for what was described as an all-star fight exhibition card that was headed by heavyweights Joe Rice of Fort Worth, Texas, and Telden Stutz of Oklahoma City, Oklahoma.

Baugh won the fight, and the *Abilene Reporter-News* reported that Tolar did the "rush act," while Baugh "let him have it with socks on the head."

After High School

At TCU, Baugh won All-American honors as a quarterback in 1935 and 1936. He finished fourth in the Heisman voting for the '36 season. Baugh also played baseball at TCU and was signed by the St. Louis Cardinals. He actually acquired the nickname "Slingin' Sammy" during his baseball career. Baugh quit baseball after several minor league seasons.

The Washington Redskins selected Baugh with the sixth overall pick in the 1937 NFL Draft. Baugh was an ironman during his rookie season, playing quarterback and defensive back. When he retired, he held thirteen league records at three positions— quarterback, punter, and defensive back.

Chase Daniel—Southlake Carroll High School—Southlake, Texas

During the 2017 NFL season, Chase Daniel was the backup quarterback to future Hall of Famer Drew Brees. However, in his high school days, Chase was one of the most prolific quarterbacks that the state of Texas had ever seen. Thanks to Todd Dodge's high-power spread offense, Daniel led the Dragons to a state championship and a runner-up finish during his two years as a starter. His overall record as a quarterback was 31–1, with the only loss coming against Katy in the 2003 Class 5A Division II championship game.

Like so many players at powerful Southlake Carroll, Daniel had to wait his turn at quarterback. As a sophomore in 2002, Daniel played wide receiver for the Dragons, who captured the state's Class 5A Division II title with a 45–14 win over Smithson Valley. Daniel caught three passes for 34 yards in the championship game.

Daniel took the reins of the high-octane Dragon offense in 2003. He led the defending champs to a 15–0 start and a second-straight berth in the state championship game. Daniel was a dual threat for opponents as he threw for 3,681 yards with 42 touchdowns and only nine interceptions while running for 1,529 and 18 touchdowns.

Katy's game plan going into the 2003 championship game was to control tempo, keeping Southlake Carroll's offense off the field. The Tigers did just that by using a clock-chewing rushing attack that allowed them to run three times more plays than the Dragons. Daniel was a perfect 6-for-6 in the passing department in the first quarter for 119 yards, including a 66-yard touchdown pass to Kenton Gedwed for a 7–0 lead after their first offensive possession. Katy won the game, 16–15, with a touchdown with two and a half minutes to go in the game that was played at the Alamodome in San Antonio.

"The key to the game was keeping Daniel and that offense off the field," said Katy head coach Gary Joseph. "Quite honestly, we needed to play a perfect game and we did."

"Out of all the quarterbacks that I've coached, Chase came the farthest," said Dodge, who during his illustrious high school coaching career has coached nine different quarterbacks who have won the Texas Offensive Player of the Year Award. "I'm very proud of what he's been able to accomplish."

During his senior season, Daniel led the Dragons back to the top of Texas high school football. Southlake Carroll finished with a perfect 16–0 mark, which was the beginning of three straight state championships for the Dragons.

The Dragons won the state title on a 41-yard field goal as time expired to beat Smithson Valley, 27–24. The winning field goal was set up by a Daniel 16-yard completion to Clint Renfro with six seconds left. Daniel, a two-time Associated Press 5A Player of the Year, finished the championship game with 290 yards passing and 89 yards rushing.

"That field goal to win it was pretty cool," said Daniel, who calls the 2004 state championship his favorite memory. "It was my dream to play for the Dragons, and I got to play under Coach Dodge. It's something I'll be proud of for the rest of my life."

Daniel ended his career with an incredible 8,298 yards passing with 91 touchdowns. He also ran for 2,954 yards and 39 touchdowns.

"I always go back to the fundamentals," said Daniel, looking back on his career. "As a quarterback, it always goes back to accuracy, so I was always working on my accuracy."

After High School

Daniel left the Lone Star State for college. He was a three-year starter at the University of Missouri, where he became the school's career total offense yards leader with 13,256.

Daniel was not selected in the 2009 NFL Draft but was signed as a free agent with the Washington Redskins though was cut before the end of training camp. He then signed on with the Saints, where he spent three seasons. After three in Kansas City, one in Philadelphia, and then back to New Orleans, Daniel signed a free agent contract with the Chicago Bears after the 2017 season.

Y. A. Tittle—Marshall High School—Marshall, Texas

It could be said that Yelberton Abraham Tittle Jr.—or Y. A. to most—was born to play the position of quarterback. Like his hero Sammy Baugh, Tittle spent hours as a young boy throwing a football through a tire swing, which led him to become one of the state's all-time top dual-threats like his hero Slingin' Sammy. Tittle said he threw balls through a tire swing because that was what he saw Baugh do in newsreels.

Tittle was born on October 24, 1926, in Marshall, Texas, a town in the northeast part of the state. Marshall has always been special to Tittle even though he left it a long time ago to start his college football career at Louisiana State University in Baton Rouge, Louisiana.

"When someone asks me where I'm from, I say Marshall, Texas," Tittle told the *Marshall News Messenger* in 2015. "My daughter or whoever is around will say, 'No, you're not. You're from California.' Then I will say, 'Well, my heart is in Marshall, Texas.'"

Tittle, who passed away in October 2017, just sixteen days shy of his ninety-first birthday, played high school football for the Marshall Mavericks during the days of leather helmets. Tittle was the Mavericks' fullback who was also known to toss the ball around a lot as well. The fact of the matter is that Y. A. was one of the best all-around players at multiple positions for the Mavs.

At the start of his football career, Y. A.'s biggest goal was to be as good as his older brother, Jack, who played for Marshall High before moving on to play at Tulane University. Jack Tittle, who was several years ahead of Y. A. at Marshall, was an All-District 11-AA back for the Mavericks.

Tittle's varsity career began as a sophomore in 1941. He wore No. 33 and was listed as weighing 180 pounds in a preseason preview in the *Marshall News Messenger*. The newspaper's Spencer Jones wrote that Tittle was one of the new players coming up from the junior high ranks. He indicated that James "Pap" Watson would be the team's quarterback but wrote that Tittle would "get his hands full" when he was on the field. In the '40s, that meant Tittle would be counted on in the passing game.

The reign of Odus Mitchell as the program's head coach began in 1941. Mitchell liked using the man-in-motion T-formation on offense.

Heading into the season opener, the *Marshall News Messenger* noted that Tittle was getting noticed for his ability to play multiple positions. In fact, there was a chance that Y. A. would be the team's starting center in the season opener against Pittsburg because of injuries to the starting and backup centers. He didn't play center, but his versatility was going to come in handy to Coach Mitchell, who considered Y. A. to be the team's handyman. Even though he was one of the youngest players on the team, he could be relied upon as he knew more plays and positions than anyone on the squad.

Tittle's talent began to shine early in the season, and Coach Mitchell put him into the line-up more and the more in the backfield. Tittle didn't disappoint, helping the Mavs to a 6–3–1 mark for the season. The Mavs were actually 6–1–1 before closing the season with two shutout losses to Longview and Tyler. At the end of the season, Tittle was named as the team's outstanding backfield performer.

Y. A. continued to improve during his junior season. However, it didn't result in more victories. Marshall finished 1942 with a 3–6–1 record, but Tittle was named second team All-District at left halfback. Between his junior and senior seasons, Tittle switched from No. 33 to No. 90.

The man who was known as the "Bald Eagle" during his NFL playing days, because of a receding hairline that began in college, had an outstanding senior season at Marshall leading the Mavericks to a district championship and a 9–2 record. The Mavs only losses that year came against Lufkin High School.

Marshall lost to Lufkin 19–7 during the regular season and then the Mavs lost 32–6 to the Panthers in the first round of the Class 2A state playoffs. Lufkin would finish runner-up in the state that year with a loss to San Angelo Central in the championship game.

While there wasn't a state championship for Marshall in 1943, there were a lot of big moments—like the season opener when Tittle and his teammates ventured to Waco. Marshall came away with a 20–6 victory, which set the tone for a regular season that saw the Mavs' offense rank among the best in the state.

Marshall ripped off five wins at the start of the 1943 season. After the Waco win, the Mavs beat Nacogdoches (40–6), Paris

(18–7), Gladewater (26–7), and Kilgore (47–7) before losing to Lufkin during the sixth week of the season.

In the win against Nacogdoches, Tittle was saluted in the *Marshall News Messenger* game report for his two touchdown runs and completing five of seven passes for 72 yards.

After losing its regular season game against Lufkin, Marshall bounced back with a 38–6 defeat of Athens. Tittle rushed for two scores and was a touted for a touchdown pass that traveled about 45 yards in the air.

In the ninth game of the regular season, Marshall played its arch-rival Longview. It's one of the oldest high school football rivalries in the Lone Star State, as the Mavericks have been playing Longview for over one hundred years. The series began in 1909 between the two schools that are about 30 miles apart.

Tittle and his teammates weren't able to beat Longview over the previous two seasons, losing 23–0 in 1941 and 28–7 in 1942, which gave the Lobos a three-game series win streak coming into the 1943 game.

While the Mavs finally beat their arch-rivals, 13–6, Tittle hurt his knee in the victory, which caused him to sit out the next game against Tyler. Tittle returned for the state playoff game against Lufkin but was hampered by the lingering injury.

Coming into the playoffs, Lufkin was ranked No. 1 in the state. Before the injury, Tittle had the offense clicking with Marshall outscoring its opponents 287–65 on the season. Lufkin beat Marshall for the second time of the year 32–6, which dropped the curtain on Y. A.'s scholastic football career.

After the season, Tittle was honored by being named to the Big Ten Honor Roll for the 25th annual All-Southern High School

Football Squad that was made up of players from twelve different states. Tittle was named to the honorable mention list along with Highland Park's Bobby Layne.

After High School

Tittle, who played offense and defense at LSU, was a tailback on offense during his first year of college football but switched to quarterback during his sophomore season. He set all of LSU's passing records in the late '40s that stood the test of time until Bert Jones broke them in the early '70s.

Tittle was the sixth overall selection in the 1948 NFL Draft by the Detroit Lions but began his pro career with the Baltimore Colts of the All-American Football Conference. Y. A. moved on to play with the San Francisco 49ers and New York Giants during his 17-year professional career. He was elected to the Pro Football Hall of Fame in 1971.

THE RUNNING BACKS

David Overstreet—Big Sandy High School— Big Sandy, Texas

David Overstreet is remembered as one of East Texas' all-time great high school football running backs. Unfortunately, Overstreet's professional career and life ended tragically on June 25, 1984, when he died in a one-car accident near Tyler, Texas. Overstreet had just finished his first year with the Miami Dolphins after playing two seasons in the Canadian Football League.

To the people of Big Sandy, David Arthur Overstreet, who was born on September 20, 1958, made Friday nights come alive every time he touched the ball.

During Overstreet's career, he ran for 7,582 yards with 102 touchdowns. He scored 56 in 1975, which places him tied for fifth in the all-time single-season record books. Overstreet's dominating performances led Big Sandy to three straight Class B state titles from 1973 to 1975.

As mentioned in the chapter on Lovie Smith, the 1975 Big Sandy team that Smith and Overstreet were teammates on was one of the best ever in America. The Wildcats outscored their opponents 824–15. The 824 points was a national record at the time, and the defense collected eleven shutouts.

"He [David] was special," said Lovie Smith. "You can't call a lot of people special, but he *was* special. He was also great on the basketball court and at running track. It didn't matter what position he played in football, he had God-given talent. Believe it or not, he played defensive end and linebacker for us…that's how good he was.

"He could do everything on the football field, because he was so smart and so confident," added Smith. "It wasn't a surprise to anyone that he'd go on the University of Oklahoma and have success and then go high in the NFL draft (No. 13 overall) because that's what a talent like his is supposed to do. When a player like that doesn't get a chance to play out his career, you just don't know how good he could have been."

There's one stat which shows you how good Overstreet was. During the 1975 season, he averaged 23.8 yards a carry. That's not a typo. The late David Overstreet averaged nearly 24 yards a carry when he was handed the ball.

After High School

Overstreet moved on to the University of Oklahoma after high school, where he played for Barry Switzer. The Miami Dolphins selected Overstreet with the 13th overall pick in the 1981 NFL Draft. However, a contract dispute led to him signing with the Montreal Alouettes of the CFL for two seasons. He returned to the states for the 1983 NFL season with the Dolphins, rushing for 392 yards on just 85 carries. He sadly lost his life in a one-car accident on June 24, 1984.

Adrian Peterson—Palestine High School— Palestine, Texas

Adrian Lewis Peterson was born on March 21, 1985, in Palestine, Texas. His parents, Bonita and Nelson Peterson, were both collegiate athletes. His dad played basketball at the University of Idaho, while his mom earned a track and field scholarship to the University of Houston after being a three-time Texas state champion at Westwood High School.

Peterson's young life wasn't the easiest, as he had to deal with his father being sent to prison after being found guilty of money laundering and witnessing his brother killed while riding a bike by a drunk driver. Adrian was actually playing football near the site of the tragic crash. After the accident, the Peterson's moved from Dallas to Palestine.

When Adrian formally began playing the game at the youth level, some say there were games where he was never tackled.

However, his high school career started with being tripped up a couple of times.

Peterson played a few varsity football games as a freshman at Westwood High School, the other high school in Palestine, but hurt his knee which required surgery and ended his season. When his family moved across town and he was enrolled in Palestine High School for his sophomore year, Adrian's grades made him ineligible to play.

"After I hurt my knee as a freshman, I didn't care about my grades, because I knew I wouldn't be playing anyway," said Peterson.

The knee injury didn't affect Peterson's speed. In the 2002 UIL Class 4A track and field championships, Peterson finished seventh in the 100-meters with a time of 10.66 seconds. The next year as a junior, Peterson improved to 10.33 seconds, placing second.

Thanks to an improvement in grades, the linebacker-sized kid with sprinter speed made his debut on the football field with the Palestine Wildcats as a junior in 2002. From the moment he stepped on the field, Peterson was unstoppable. His all-time favorite memory actually came in his very first game with the Wildcats, in the team's season opener against Huntsville High School.

"I ran for over 300 yards in that game and scored four touchdowns," recalled Peterson. "It was a great start to the season for me."

The exact numbers for the Huntsville game were 340 yards on 22 carries with four touchdowns in the Wildcats' 40–12 victory.

Peterson finished his junior year averaging 8.3 yards per carry while rushing for 2,051 yards with 22 touchdowns.

After an 8–2 regular season, Palestine advanced to the Class 4A Division II playoffs for the first time since 1994. They would go on to beat Kilgore 13–6 in the opening round. Peterson was a workhorse, carrying the ball 34 times for 256 yards and scoring both Wildcat touchdowns. However, Palestine's state championship dreams ended the following weekend with a 33–20 loss to Waco's University High.

Peterson's outstanding junior year was the springboard to an incredible senior season that saw him ascend to be the No. 1 football recruit in the country. Peterson rushed for 2,960 yards and averaged 11.7 yards per carry while scoring 32 touchdowns.

Once again, the Wildcats qualified for the postseason after a 9–1 regular season, but things came to a quick halt in the playoffs when Hallsville upset them, 20–19, in the first round. Peterson's last high school football game featured a fast start that saw the future University of Oklahoma star score three first-half touchdowns to give Palestine a 19–7 halftime lead. After running for 136 yards in the first half, the Hallsville defense held Peterson to 90 yards in the second half and kept him out of the end zone.

One of the interesting things about Peterson is how he always wanted to play defense, but his coaches didn't want to risk injury to their star tailback on that side of the ball.

"I really enjoyed playing high school football," said Peterson. "It gave me the basis for everything I've achieved since those days. Mostly, it taught me about working hard to achieve goals."

After High School

Peterson played at Oklahoma from 2004 to 2006, during which time he ran for 4,041 yards while averaging 5.4 yards per carry with 41 touchdowns. During his freshman season, Peterson finished second in the Heisman Trophy voting to USC quarterback Matt Leinart.

The Minnesota Vikings drafted Peterson with the seventh overall pick in the 2007 NFL Draft. Heading into the 2018 season, Peterson ranks 12th on the NFL's all-time rushing yardage list.

THE RECEIVERS

Dez Bryant—Lufkin High School—Lufkin, Texas

Does Dez Bryant love his hometown of Lufkin? The answer is a resounding yes.

Before Bryant headed to the Dallas Cowboys' fall training camp in Oxnard, California, in 2017, he headed back to his East Texas hometown to put on a barbecue for the *entire* town. Yes, Bryant's party, which included various activities, was for every single person in the community of 16,000.

Bryant invited residents with a simple post on his Facebook page:

> *I'll be in Lufkin tomorrow...BBQ...Drinks all on me...also I want to play kick ball so we need to form some teams...I'm trying to figure out which park has the most space to set all of this up at... any suggestions on parks hit my inbox...trying to have fun before I head back to camp...*
>
> *EVERYONE free to join*
> *Share this post*

At the event, Bryant said, "I'm at a loss for words just to see all these people showing this support. But this is why I do it. I do it for y'all. This means so much to me. Y'all the only reason I go. Y'all are my engine I promise. I'm going to let people know Lufkin is No. 1 in my heart. You people are No. 1 in my heart. That's not going to change."

The event, which cost him $13,000, was held at Kit McConnico Park and dubbed "Family Fun Day," and also included free haircuts for grade school kids.

Why did he do it?

"I'm nothing without those people," said Bryant.

Desmond Demond Bryant was born on November 8, 1988, in Galveston County, Texas. His family eventually moved to Lufkin in East Texas, where the Lufkin Panthers have been a high school football power in that part of the state for a long time.

"Dez was the biggest secret in Lufkin," said Oscar Kennedy, who coached Bryant's 7-on-7 passing league team during his high school days. "I remember him playing JV football and he was an awesome specimen. He had the biggest hands of any kid that size that I had ever seen. Always playful, easy going, and would give you the shirt off his back.

"I remember Dez in the playoffs during his sophomore season," recalled Kennedy. "We had a great season. We were undefeated and played one of those great Southlake Carroll teams with head coach Todd Dodge. I remember Coach Dodge saying after the game, 'Where the heck did he [Dez] come from?'"

"What I remember is that when we saw Dez on film in the quarterfinal game from the week before, he was wearing Number 48," recalled Todd Dodge, who led Southlake Carroll to four

state titles. "I remember saying 'Who's that good-looking sophomore receiver?' He hadn't played during the regular season, so it
was our first look at him. Thank goodness we got a look at him
on film from the week before, because you could tell he was special. That's how good Lufkin was that season…Dez Bryant didn't
play on varsity during the regular season."

Bryant caught a 28-yard touchdown pass with about six minutes to go in that game to tie the score at 30–30, which brought
the Panthers all the way back from a 27–9 halftime deficit. Southlake Carroll ended up winning the game, 37–30.

Lufkin again lost to Southlake Carroll in 2005, 46–28, which
was the third straight season that the Panthers were knocked out
of the playoffs during the state semifinals by the Dragons who
ended up winning three straight Class 5A state titles.

Reports from the game indicate that the Lufkin's passing game
struggled that day, with Bryant leading the team with five catches
for 65 yards and two touchdowns.

As a junior, Bryant caught 48 passes for 1,025 yards with 16
touchdowns, which helped him catch the eye of major college
football programs from around the nation. He closed out his
scholastic career with 52 catches for 1,027 yards with 21 touchdowns. Bryant made All-State that year, plus was named a *Parade*
magazine All-American.

In his two years as a starter, Bryant caught 101 passes for 2,232
yards with 37 touchdowns.

"I really did enjoy my high school days and the coaches that
helped shape my life," said Bryant, who actually held his Pro Day
for the NFL scouts before the draft in Lufkin. "That Pro Day was
very exciting and scary at the same time because there were so

many NFL teams there, but on the other hand, I got to do it in my hometown that I love."

After High School

The four-star recruit, who was ranked as the nation's No. 9 receiving prospect, chose Oklahoma State University. During his sophomore year, he led OSU with 87 catches and 19 touchdowns, earning him All-American honors. After being ruled ineligible by the NCAA three games into his junior year, Bryant entered the 2010 NFL Draft. The Dallas Cowboys took Bryant as the 24th overall pick. Through the 2017 season, Bryant has 909 career catches for over 7,400 yards with 73 touchdowns.

Johnny "Lam" Jones—Lampasas High School— Lampasas, Texas

Johnny Jones, the kid who won an Olympic gold medal at the age of seventeen in the Montreal Summer Olympics, is a Texas legend. In a day-and-age long before the NFL Combine, Jones had straight-line speed that was compared to lightning. From media reports in the late '70s, it was said that Jones once ran a 40-yard dash in 4.34 seconds, but Jones said his best time was 4.23 seconds. To put that in perspective, John Ross of the Cincinnati Bengals set the NFL combine record in 2017 with a time of 4.22 seconds. No matter what the era, the young man from Lampasas could flat-out run.

Johnny Wesley Jones was born on April 4, 1958, in Lawton, Oklahoma, and began playing football in the third grade. He would spend his summers with his grandparents in Lampasas, Texas, before moving there permanently with them in the seventh grade. Lampasas is a small town of about 6,000 people that is pretty much right in the center of the Lone Star State.

"I really enjoyed playing football in Lawton," said Jones. "We had some really good players. Vaughn Lusby was a couple years older than me and he was really good. He played cornerback at Arkansas where he was an All-American. Our team in Oklahoma won the Pop Warner championship three years in a row."

Jones said that he's always been a team player in any sport that he played. He said because of that, he doesn't recall a lot of individual stuff during his time on the football field.

"I've always been shy," Jones said. "The best part of sports is coming together with your teammates and coaches to achieve something special."

Jones said he got a few starts as a sophomore on Lampasas' varsity squad that went 3–7 in District 12-AAA in 1973. While Jones may not remember a lot of individual moments, a review of newspapers from the 1974 and 1975 season shows some of his outstanding moments.

After being knocked out of the first game in the first quarter in 1974, Jones bounced back with an outstanding effort against Fredericksburg. The speedy back, operating out of the wishbone formation, carried the ball nine times for 197 yards and four touchdowns. For those of you without a calculator, that's an average of 21.9 yards per carry.

He put up a similar performance against Llano High when he carried the ball only twelve times for 154 yards and four touchdowns. For the season, Jones ran for 1,330 yards and averaged 11.6 yards per carry, which landed him a spot on the second team of the Class AAA All-State squad that was chosen by the Texas Sports Writers Association. Jones scored 159 points for the year.

The numbers kept growing during Jones's senior season. In a game against Gainesville, he shredded the defense for 257 yards and four touchdowns. Jones had an outstanding senior season, finishing his career with 45 touchdowns and a spot on the first team of the Texas Sports Writers Association's All-State football team.

Jones was inducted into the Texas High School Football Hall of Fame in 2008.

After High School

Before heading to the University of Texas, Jones headed north of the border to participate in the 1976 Summer Olympics in Montreal, Canada. Jones replaced Houston McTear, who was injured and couldn't participate. As a seventeen-year-old, Jones finished sixth in the 100-meters and then won a gold medal running the second leg of the 4x100-meter relay.

As a member of the Texas Longhorns football team, Johnny picked up his nickname "Lam." On that same team was another Johnny Jones, which led head coach Fred Akers to name them after their hometowns. Akers decided on Johnny "Lam" Jones from Lampasas, and Johnny "Ham" Jones from Hamlin. Johnny Lam's college career began as a running back before he was moved to wide receiver. He averaged 28 catches per year but averaged over 18.9 yards per grab.

Jones's speed was a huge attraction to NFL teams, which led to him being selected as the No. 2 overall pick in the 1980 NFL

Draft by the New York Jets. He signed a $2.1 million contract, which was the largest ever for a wide receiver at that time.

THE LINEMEN

Forrest Gregg—Sulphur Springs High School—Sulphur Springs, Texas

Alvis Forrest Gregg was born on October 18, 1933, in Birthright, Texas, which is just north of Sulphur Springs. Gregg, one of eleven children born to David Boyd and Josephine Gregg, attended Sulphur Springs High School where he excelled in four sports: basketball, baseball, football, and track and field.

Gregg, who's been known by his middle name since he was young, had a tough upbringing as one of eleven children working on a tiny farm in Birthright. At the age of fifteen, he moved on his own ten miles south to Sulphur Springs where he began his sports career. In his autobiography *Winning in the Trenches: A Lifetime of Football*, Gregg said he was always thinking about sports as a youngster.

After moving to Sulphur Springs to play freshman football, legend has it that Gregg didn't even know how to properly put on his uniform. During his sophomore season, Gregg played in a scrimmage against Paris High School. As mentioned earlier, that game featured Gregg and Raymond Berry, who both landed in Pro Football's Hall of Fame in Canton.

Few stats were kept on linemen back then, but Gregg's bio on the Texas High School Football Hall of Fame website states that he "was so good that enemy game plans always stated in bold letters, 'DON'T RUN PLAYS AT THE BIG TACKLE.'"

In 2013, Gregg, who has been battling Parkinson's disease, was honored for his days in Sulphur Springs when the Pro Football Hall of Fame teamed-up with Allstate Insurance for the Hometown Hall of Famers program, which honored the hometown roots of the sport's greatest coaches, players, and contributors with special ceremonies at their respective high schools.

During Gregg's ceremony, he told the crowd that every part of his success linked back to Sulphur Springs. "Whatever I have achieved links back to this town and this high school," he said. "From the people who befriended me, gave me a place to live, and gave me a job and direction…I want to thank each and every one of you."

After High School

Gregg attended Southern Methodist University after graduating from Sulphur Springs. The Green Bay Packers picked Gregg in the second round of the 1956 NFL Draft. He won five NFL championships as a member of the Packers before closing out his career with Dallas (where he won another title when the Cowboys beat the Miami Dolphins in Super Bowl VI). Gregg is one of only three players in professional football history to win six world championships, and he was elected to the Hall of Fame in 1977.

After his playing days, Gregg went into coaching, serving as an NFL head coach with the Cleveland Browns, Cincinnati Bengals, and Green Bay. He led Cincinnati to Super Bowl XVI, where the Bengals lost to the San Francisco 49ers, 26–21.

He also was a head coach in the Canadian Football League with two teams and was head coach at his alma mater SMU for two seasons.

Jerry Sisemore—Plainview High School— Plainview, Texas

Plainview, Texas, wasn't the biggest town in the Lone Star State in the '60s, with a little less than 20,000 residents. However, the Plainview Bulldogs football team put the West Texas town on the map by placing three former players in the NFL, led by College Football Hall of Famer Jerry Sisemore. During the 1967 through 1969 seasons, Sisemore, who played his entire professional career with the Philadelphia Eagles, teamed up with future NFL Pro Bowl running back Lawrence McCutcheon.

Jerald Grant Sisemore was born on July 16, 1951, in Olten, Texas. Jerry never truly thought about playing football—in fact, as a young boy, he was destined to be in the marching band.

"The seventh-grade football coach at Coronado Junior High came walking by the band hall and I was over in the corner hiding behind my trombone," recalled Sisemore. "I did not want to do that [play football], because I knew it was going to be tough and I wanted to play the trombone. I loved music. Coach said, 'No, no, no, you're coming with me.'"

And that's how Sisemore's music career ended and his football career began in West Texas. Sisemore said that he was a chubby kid when he was young, standing about 5-foot-2 and weighing 153 pounds in the fifth grade. By the time he was a freshman at Plainview High School, he had grown to 6-foot-4 and weighed 190 pounds. Eventually, Sisemore said he "bulked up to 210."

Back in the late '60s, the Plainview football program wasn't all that good. In fact, the Bulldogs hadn't had a winning season in nearly a quarter of a century.

"We were classified with all of the Lubbock schools and all of the Amarillo schools," said Sisemore. "Then you throw in Pampa and Borger and we were the redheaded stepchild. Those teams just slapped us all over the place."

After playing on the Plainview freshman team, Sisemore was moved up to varsity during his sophomore season. He played on both sides of the ball as an offensive and defensive lineman.

However, the arrival of the future College Football Hall of Famer and NFLer didn't change Plainview's success. The Bulldogs finished 1–8–1 in 1996.

Things changed during Sisemore's junior season.

"That's when Lawrence McCutcheon arrived," said Sisemore. "He was 6-foot-4, 220 pounds. He was fast and strong and one of the most amazing men I've been around. He was definitely one of my heroes in town growing up."

McCutcheon was a senior in 1967 but was well-known in the community because of his exploits playing at the all-black Booker T. Washington High School in Plainview. When BTW was closed heading into his senior year, McCutcheon joined Sisemore and his teammates to change Plainview's football fortunes.

Sisemore said that he and his teammates immediately accepted McCutcheon. "It was a beautiful time. There really were no racial issues and if there were, I never knew about them. He made a huge difference on the field. We earned a whole lot of respect and, quite honestly, it was really the beginning of the program turning around."

Plainview finished 1967 with a 7–3 record thanks to McCutcheon and Co. McCutcheon, who went on to star at Colorado State and then become an NFL All-Pro running back, finished with

589 yards rushing for the season. In 2005, McCutcheon was inducted into the Panhandle Sports Hall of Fame.

As for Sisemore and his teammates, they were able to carry their success into the 1968 season.

"Back then there was nothing to follow…no tradition…but we didn't want to be slapped around anymore," said Sisemore about getting ready for his senior season. "We were a close group with some really good football players and we decided we were *really* tired of this Lubbock/Amarillo slapping that we were getting and why not just be the one slapping them.

"Then we started beating them and we believed that we could beat them," Sisemore added. "That's when the whole thing turned direction."

Jerry said that all the coaches at Plainview were great men who cared about the kids. Don Williams was Plainview's head coach during Sisemore's sophomore year. Bill Davis took over the reins of the Bulldogs' program the following year in 1967.

"Throughout my career, at all levels, I had wonderfully adjusted coaches that I could look up to," Sisemore said. "We had real solid role models in Plainview and that was a direct reflection on the community."

After High School

Jerry attended the University of Texas where he began playing on the offensive line as a sophomore in 1970. Sisemore became the nation's best offensive lineman, being named All-America as both a junior and senior. During his time with the Longhorns, the school won three straight Southwest Conference championships.

The Philadelphia Eagles selected Sisemore with the third over-all pick in the first round of the 1973 NFL Draft. He played all twelve professional seasons with the Eagles, which included playing in Super Bowl XV where the team lost to the Oakland Raiders.

In 2002, Sisemore was elected to the College Football Hall of Fame.

"There's no doubt in my mind that Jerry Sisemore is one of the best offensive tackles to ever play the game of football," said Ken Dabbs, former University of Texas recruiting coordinator and assistant coach.

20

Defensive Players

AS THE SAYING goes, defense wins championships. Just ask Pittsburgh Steelers fans what Temple's "Mean Joe" Greene meant to his team during the run to four Super Bowl titles. In this chapter, several of the Lone Star State's best reminisce about their days stuffing running backs and quarterbacks while preventing completions and forcing turnovers.

DEFENSIVE LINEMEN

Brad Shearer—Westlake High School—Austin, Texas

Sterling Bradford Shearer was born on August 10, 1955, in Houston, Texas. Like Earl Campbell and Elmo Wright, Shearer is a disciple of the Ken Dabbs's way of football.

In 1970, Shearer was a freshman at Austin's Reagan High School, which was in the middle of an incredible run during the late '60s. Under head coach Travis Raven, the Raiders won state titles in 1967, 1968, and again at the end of the 1970 season. Reagan missed out on the playoffs in 1969 with an 8–2 record. During that four-year stretch, the Raiders were 51–3.

"The freshman team went undefeated that year, the JV went undefeated, and we won state," recounted Shearer. "Unfortunately, the next year, we moved back to Houston. I went to Lee High School and was starting both ways. I was all suited up for the first game when I was ruled ineligible."

Brad and his mom returned to the Austin area for his junior year, but this time he was at Westlake High School that had just opened in 1969. Unlike his freshman year when he played at Austin Reagan, which was a 4A school, Westlake was a smaller 2A school. The head coach at Westlake was none other than Ken Dabbs, who was brought in to start the Chaparrals' football program from scratch.

Coach Dabbs is old school, meaning he had some strict rules—like players couldn't have long hair. Big Brad, who weighed around 220 pounds, had long hair *and* rode a motorcycle.

"It was the '70s," Shearer chuckled. "The first time I met Coach Dabbs he didn't mention my hair. He just wanted me to practice. I'll never forget that they didn't have shoes that fit me… they didn't have shoulder pads that fit…the helmet *did* fit, but they didn't have pants that fit me.

"They did get me suited up, and by the time I got out on the field, they were running 220s. I hadn't worked out a whole lot that year, so I was struggling a bit and after we had finished running a couple of them Coach asked me, 'So what do you think?' I said, 'Coach, I've never run 220 yards to tackle or block anybody…do you think we can knock that down a little bit to maybe 50 yards?' He told me that he'd think about it and the very next day we were only running 50s."

"Early on, I remember one of our counselors wanted me to meet Brad and that person told me to look at his feet and not his hair," laughed Coach Dabbs. "Well, when I met him, I liked what I saw. He was big! I knew he was riding a motorcycle, so the first thing I told him was that he couldn't ride the motorcycle anymore, which he agreed to do. I didn't say anything about his hair."

A couple of days into practice, Shearer said he still had his long hair, but everybody else on the team had their buzz cuts. Shearer still had his long locks when the team scrimmaged Gonzalez High School.

"We put Brad in at defensive tackle for some goal line work," recalled Dabbs. "They were at the 10-yard line and kept running at Brad and nine plays later, they were still at the 10! He was running all over the field making tackles.

"After the scrimmage, my coaches came into the office to tell me that we had a problem. Around the same time, three players came into the office asking what I was going to do with the big guy and the long hair. I told them that maybe I was going to grow my hair."

Shearer did cut his hair in time for the team's first pep rally, and the rest was history. Shearer became one of the top linemen in the state of Texas.

After High School

Coach Dabbs left Westlake after Shearer's junior year to become an assistant coach at the University of Texas. When Dabbs became the Longhorns' recruiting coordinator, he brought in Shearer who would start at defensive tackle as a freshman. During his senior year, Shearer won the Outland Trophy, which is given to college football's top interior lineman.

The Chicago Bears took Shearer in the third round of the 1978 NFL Draft. He played with the Bears from 1978 to 1981, but his professional career was cut short by a knee injury.

Gene Stallings—Paris High School—Paris, Texas

Gene Stallings loves Paris, Texas. After forty years of coaching college and professional football around the country, the College Football Hall of Famer retired to his ranch in his hometown of Paris.

Eugene Clifton Stallings Jr. was born on March 2, 1935, in Paris. And, just like Raymond Berry, Stallings enjoyed growing up in the northEast Texas town about 100 miles northeast of the Dallas-Fort Worth Metroplex.

"The stadium was always full," reminisced Stallings, whose family nickname is Bebes. "There was lots of excitement. I remember dressing at our practice facility and then busing over to the stadium. We had good teams during my time there...not great, but we always won seven or eight games but never got to the state playoffs.

"In Paris, Texas, if Coach Berry said it, that was the rule. He had great respect from the people in Paris and everyone wanted to play for him. He was a technique coach and had philosophies that I carried into my own coaching career."

The 1950 season marked the thirteenth for the elder Berry, who had a .768 winning percentage with 113 wins against only 36 losses with 11 ties. In his first dozen years, the Wildcats had won five district championships.

Stallings was moved up to the varsity team after playing on the B Team his freshman year. The B Team was the equivalent of a JV team. He said playing in Noyes Stadium was always a treat for him. Even as a sophomore, the local newspaper touted how good a defensive end he was. In fact, by the time he was a junior, Coach Berry was calling him one of the greatest ends. After his junior season, a year in which the two-way starter also had six touchdown catches, Stallings was named to the first team 3-AAA All-District.

"I remember one thing about my high school career was Coach Berry always liked to beat Denison," recalled Stallings.

The local newspaper referred to the Paris-Denison rivalry as a "feud." From the 1942 season, four of eleven games were decided by less than a touchdown with two ties. The 1952 game was a heartbreaker for Stallings and his head coach as Denison scored with 25 seconds left to play in the game in a 7–0 loss for the Wildcats.

One of Stallings's better games as a senior came on November 8, 1952, when he caught six passes for 145 yards and a touchdown in a 39–0 shutout of Greenville.

"The only other game I truly remember was the game against McKinney. It was so cold, and I remember breaking through on a punt and thinking to myself that I was going to break my hands off if I blocked it. I did, but boy did it sting," laughed Stallings.

Stallings was named to the All-District Team after his senior season, plus second team Class AAA All-State. He was also touted for his ability to win a coin toss at the start of the game. Midway through the 1952 season, the *Paris News* indicated that "Bebes" was a perfect 6-for-6 on tosses.

"Back then, we went from sport to sport, so your real camaraderie was with your teammates," said Stallings. "No matter whenever I came back to town years later, I would always seek out my old teammates, because we really bonded with each other."

After High School

Stallings went to play his college football at Texas A&M where, under Paul "Bear" Bryant, he became one of the "Junction Boys." In 1965, at the age of twenty-nine, he became the head coach at his alma mater. Stallings was the head coach of the NFL's St. Louis/Arizona Cardinals from 1986 through 1989. In 1992, he led the University of Alabama to a perfect 13–0 season and a national championship.

LINEBACKERS

Jessie Armstead—Carter High School—Dallas, Texas

The 1991 Dallas Carter High School football team was one of the best ever, with five future NFL players on the roster. For those of you not familiar with the team, it's the one that was immortalized in Peter Berg's film *Friday Night Lights*. Hollywood fictionalized the 1988 season by having Carter beat Odessa Permian High School in the Class 5A championship game, instead of the historically accurate state semifinals, but it didn't take away from how good the Cowboys were that season. As mentioned earlier (in the Derwin Gray chapter), Carter beat Converse Judson 31–14 for the state title in 1988. At the heart of that Carter team that was eventually stripped of the state title in 1990 for using academically ineligible players during the '88 season was linebacker Jessie Armstead.

Jessie Willard Armstead was born on October 26, 1970, in Dallas, Texas. He grew up in the Oak Cliff section of Dallas that was considered middle-class. He said that growing up he was able to avoid the pitfalls of some of the things going on around him in the neighborhood. Maybe that's why Armstead was able to say no to teammates who approached him about taking part in a burglary ring that included six Carter football teammates that were linked to twenty-one robberies that began five days after Carter won its '88 state championship.

Armstead was a man among boys on the football field. He was a three-time high school All-American. How exclusive of a club is that? At the time, Armstead was the *only* member. At 6-foot-3 and 205 pounds, he had a body that looked like God made him to play linebacker.

Jessie was the inspirational leader of the Carter defense, which struck fear in the hearts of opponents. The '88 season saw the Cowboys shutout six opponents and only gave up 117 points all season. Carter finished 14–0–1, with the only blemish on their record being a 24–24 tie against Duncanville.

"I always wanted to make the guy next to me believe in himself more than he was supposed to believe in himself," said Armstead. "I believe our team was the best ever in high school football."

"When we played Armstead in the 1988 championship game, we didn't know whether to run at him or run away from him," said D. W. Rutledge, head coach of Judson High School. "We decided to run at him because he had so much speed, but it didn't make any difference. He was stuffing us no matter what we were doing. You do try to game plan around some of those guys that are that talented, but remember, he had so many other guys around him, so there weren't a lot of options. We just couldn't match up with Armstead and the rest of them, because of their overall team speed."

Armstead said the best thing about that team is all of the players grew up together, which made the accomplishment that much greater.

After High School

Armstead attended the University of Miami (Florida), where he played on the 1989 and 1991 national championship teams. The New York Giants drafted him in the eighth round of the 1993 NFL Draft. Armstead was a five-time Pro Bowler with the Giants, while also playing with the Washington Redskins and Carolina Panthers.

Von Miller—DeSoto High School—DeSoto, Texas

There aren't many No. 2 picks in the NFL Draft that are willing to call themselves a nerd, but that's just how Von Miller of the Denver Broncos describes his childhood.

"It's true, I was a nerd," said Miller. "A total nerd."

Vonnie B'Vsean Miller Jr. was on born March 26, 1989, in DeSoto, Texas, a suburb of Dallas that loves its high school football team, which has produced more than a dozen NFL players. Miller recalls that he first wanted to play football in the fifth grade, but his father said he wasn't ready, so the only way he could go out for the peewee team was to get his mom to say yes and then keep it their little secret.

Miller's fifth-grade team only had eleven players, so everyone played both ways. That fifth-grade team turned out to be pretty good, finishing the regular season undefeated, according to a story he wrote for *The Players Tribune* in 2016. People in the community that knew Miller realized that he was very focused on being a football player that would go to the next level.

In 2005, as a junior, Miller showed everyone that he was a next-level player with 37 tackles and seven sacks, 14 of which were for a loss. He also had a dozen quarterback hurries for the Eagles. Desoto finished the regular season 6–4 and was knocked out of the Class 5A Division II playoffs with a 17–14 loss in the first round.

Miller's college stock continued to rise during his senior season when he recorded 51 solo tackles with six sacks and eleven hurries. DeSoto finished 10–4 in 2006, advancing to the state quarterfinals against arch-rival Cedar Hill. DeSoto had also lost to the Longhorns 30–27 in double overtime during the regular season. Cedar Hill went on to win the Class 5A Division II state title that year.

"Von doesn't forget where he came from," said Larry Davis, DeSoto's athletic director. "He mentions DeSoto a lot."

After High School

Miller accepted a scholarship to Texas A&M where, during his junior season, he led the nation with 17 sacks. The Denver Broncos selected Miller second overall in the 2011 NFL Draft. He was named Most Valuable Player of Super Bowl 50 with 2.5 sacks and two forced fumbles as the Broncos beat the heavily favored Carolina Panthers 24–10.

Tommy Nobis—Thomas Jefferson High School— San Antonio, Texas

Here's a trivia question: Which was the first high school team in America to have two players taken in the same NFL Draft? The answer is San Antonio's Thomas Jefferson High School.

It happened in 1966 when the Atlanta Falcons drafted linebackers Tommy Nobis and Bill Goss, who graduated from Jefferson High in 1962. Nobis was taken with the overall No. 1 pick, while Goss was picked in the eighth round.

● ● ●

Thomas Henry Nobis Jr. was born on September 20, 1943, in San Antonio, Texas. When Nobis passed away in December

2017, many remembered him as one of the game's most ferocious hitters who struck fear in opponents at every level of the game.

In an October 18, 1965, *Sports Illustrated* article called "There's No Show Biz Like Nobis," it was noted that Nobis "got up at 5:30 every morning, rode a bus, transferred, rode another, then walked, just to attend Thomas Jefferson High even though another school was located only a few blocks from his home." The San Antonio Independent School District didn't have boundaries, which is why Nobis was able to choose his school.

One of the main reasons that Nobis chose Jefferson was because of the school's head football coach, Pat Shannon. During Shannon's nine years at Jefferson, the school reportedly was awarded more college football scholarships than any school in America.

In a 2015 YouTube video that was produced by the San Antonio ISD for Nobis's induction into the school district's Hall of Fame, Nobis said another reason was he really wanted a letterman jacket with the "J" on it.

"I saw these young men walking around with jackets on. It's a thing that you'd wear around school and be very proud. Some guys would actually get their jacket and give it to their girlfriend, but I didn't do that. I kept my jacket," chuckled Nobis.

Nobis was a two-way performer at Jefferson, playing offensive end and middle linebacker. And, while Nobis was ultimately known for his bone-jarring tackles, he actually began his high school career as a 150-pound quarterback. However, between his sophomore and junior years, Nobis gained 35 pounds and moved to middle linebacker.

Nobis got his letterman jacket after his junior year and closed out his high school career winning all-state honors as a middle linebacker and offensive end.

The 1961 team made the Class 4A playoffs, beating San Antonio Brackenridge 41–7, but lost 26–7 to Corpus Christi in the quarterfinals. During Nobis's senior season, Jefferson didn't qualify for the postseason, but Brackenridge, the team Jefferson had beaten the year before, won the state's Class 4A title.

How much did Nobis love high school football? It's widely reported that whenever he visited San Antonio, he'd visit Alamo Stadium, where a plaque hangs in his honor. If the gates were locked, he would just stand outside.

"Even if it's locked, I'll stand at one of the entrances and just look through the wire gate," Nobis said a few years ago. "All the great memories come back."

DEFENSIVE BACKS

Darrell Green—Jones High School—Houston, Texas

Darrell Ray Green was born on February 15, 1960, in Houston, Texas, and is another Texan whose high school football career started late. Green was a track star a Jones High School and only played two years of high school football, making the junior varsity team as a junior and then the varsity team as a senior.

In a 1984 interview with the *New York Times*, Green said, "I was bombarded as a kid for being small. When I was in the seventh grade, the coaches put me on the sixth-grade team. I only played two years of football before I made the varsity in my senior year of high school."

However, that one year was enough to land Green a scholarship from Texas A&I. As a senior, Green was All-City as a cornerback, his only year as a varsity player. He was All-State in track but said he was always a football player first.

So how did Green go from a skinny, short, but fast football player to the Pro Football Hall of Fame cornerback? Track is the answer. Green used his speed to catch the eyes of the school's football coaches. In 2010, it was reported that on his fiftieth birthday, Green ran a 4.43 40-yard dash.

"Everybody said you're too little, you can't do it," said Green during his 2008 Hall of Fame induction ceremony in Canton. "He [Green's late dad Leonard Green] said you *can* run that ball. They said no, he said go."

Once Green's coach at Jones, James Humphries, inserted him at cornerback, the road to Canton was underway. During multiple email exchanges, Green repeatedly said he didn't have many memories from his days on the Jones High School football team.

Instead, he stuck with his words from his Hall of Fame induction speech when he said, "Quick shout-out to Jesse H. Jones High School and community. To young people in that community, this is what you can do. This is what you can do."

After High School

After his time at Texas A&I, Green was selected 28th overall in the first round of the 1983 NFL Draft. Green played his entire 20-year career with the Washington Redskins, and was inducted into the Pro Football Hall of Fame in 2008. He holds the NFL records for most consecutive seasons with an interception (19) and most games played by a defensive player (295).

Charles Tillman–Copperas Cove High School—
Copperas Cove, Texas

Like RGIII, Charles Tillman played football at Copperas Cove because his father was in the military and was stationed at nearby Fort Hood.

Charles Anthony Tillman was born on February 23, 1981, in Chicago, Illinois, but spent a lot of his time traveling the world with his father Donald Tillman Jr., who was a sergeant in the US Army. After attending eleven schools across the United States and in Germany, Tillman settled in Copperas Cove during his time in junior high.

Jack Welch, who recently retired as the head coach at Copperas Cove after over two decades, said it didn't take long to know that Tillman was special. "His freshman year, he was clearly outstanding. There was no doubt about the fact that he was going to be special. He was the best football player, the best basketball player, and he was a good trackster.

"Between his freshman and sophomore years, he thought he might go straight basketball," continued Welch. "I'll never forget talking to him in my office and I told him that he was cutting himself short...you can play both sports and be a hoss. You're going to get bigger and stronger by hitting the weights and being involved in football. I told him it would make him more marketable. I told him to give himself one more year and I think he's pretty proud that he gave himself that one more year," chuckled Welch.

Welch added that, like RGIII, Tillman was a natural leader from day one. However, the guy who was given the nickname

Peanut by his aunt because his body resembled the shape of peanut when he was young, wasn't a defensive star with the Bulldawgs.

Tillman mostly played wide receiver in high school, with Welch only using him on defense in goal-line or short-yardage situations.

"He could have gone both ways the whole time, but we tried to keep him fresh," said Welch. "Even though we only used him in certain situations, he was still our best defensive back."

After High School

Tillman was a four-year starter at the University of Lousiana at Lafayette from 1999 to 2002. The Chicago Bears selected him with the 35th overall pick in the second round of the 2003 NFL Draft. He played 13 years in the NFL, twelve of them with the Bears where he holds the team record with nine defensive touchdowns.

21

Lone Star State Legends

WITH THE ODDS of making it to the NFL against a high school football player, it stands to reason that Texas would have a large number of outstanding individual performances that didn't result in playing on Sundays...but that doesn't mean they don't deserve mentioning. In this chapter, we're going to hear from some players that had performances that made them Lone Star State high school football legends.

KEN DABBS—FREER HIGH SCHOOL—FREER, TEXAS

I've mentioned Ken Dabbs throughout this book because as the recruiting coordinator at the University of Texas he touched so many parts of Texas high school football. Every person that I talked with about Coach Dabbs said the same thing: he doesn't forget a thing, and he knows everyone.

Dabbs was born in Ranger, Texas, but moved with his family to Freer, which is south of San Antonio. He attended Freer High School where he played baseball, football, and tennis in the early '50s. Dabbs played quarterback for the Buckaroos. He said he only weighed 129 pounds as a senior.

"College football was out of the question at that size," laughed Dabbs, who went on to get his degree from Sam Houston State University.

Dabbs began making his mark on Texas high school football when he was hired as the junior high school coach at Belleville High School in the mid-'50s. He said that the entire program only had three coaches. During his time at Bellville, he coached running back Ernie Koy, who would go on to play on the University of Texas' 1963 national championship team before playing six years in the NFL with the New York Giants.

In 1958, Dabbs was hired by Sweeny High School on the Gulf Coast to become the football program's ninth-grade coach. A year later, in addition to his football coaching duties, he became the school's head track coach, winning seven district track titles in seven years, plus four regional titles. By the mid-'60s, Dabbs was Sweeny's offensive coordinator. As noted earlier, he coached Elmo Wright on Sweeny's 1966 state championship team. A year later, Dabbs and the Bulldogs advanced to the 2A quarterfinals where they lost to eventual state runner-up San Antonio Randolph, 12–7.

Dabbs's ascension through the high school ranks was swift after that. He was hired as an assistant at Irving High School for the 1967 season, and then elevated to head coach for the 1968 season. His quarterback was Alan Lowry, who would go on to become a two-sport star in baseball and football at the University of Texas before becoming a longtime NFL assistant coach with two Super Bowl rings.

The jump from a 2A team to a 4A squad didn't affect Dabbs in his first job as a head coach. After two games during the 1968 season, the Tigers were ranked No. 11 in the state. Not bad for a team that was predicted to finish third in its district that season. Irving finished the regular season with a 9–1 record, with the only loss coming against Garland High School.

With Lowry running Dabbs's Veer offense to perfection, Irving advanced to the postseason. The Tigers' opened with back-to-back victories in the playoffs. Through the first two rounds of playoffs, Lowery had rushed for 879 yards and had thrown for 915 yards. Irving lost to eventual state runner-up Odessa Permian 10–6 in the state quarterfinals to finish 11–2. That eleven-win season hasn't been equaled since.

"He was so much fun to play for," said Lowry. "He made everyone want to be out there on the field. Fifty years later, even though he was the head coach for only one year, he's still *the* guy at Irving."

"That was a great team," said Dabbs, who left Irving to start the Westlake High School program in 1969. Yes, the same Westlake program that produced Drew Brees, Nick Foles, and Outland Trophy winner Brad Shearer. Dabbs coached Shearer during his junior year with the Chaps, and he said that guys like Shearer, Earl Campbell, and Lowry are the reason he's had such a great coaching career.

"Those guys are special to me," said Dabbs. "Really great players can make a coach look really, really good—and that's what they did for me."

"When he mentioned me in the same breath as Earl Campbell, I was taken a little aback," confessed Brad Shearer. "He's been around so many good ones, so when he told me that I had an impact on his life and career, it gave me goosebumps."

Dabbs's only losing season as a coach came during Westlake's first season of varsity football in 1970 when the Chaparrals finished 2–8. After that first season, Dabbs was a winner until Texas Longhorn head coach Darrell Royal came calling. Royal hired Dabbs to be his running backs coach, but he quickly elevated him to be the Longhorns' recruiting coordinator in charge of bringing Earl Campbell to Austin.

"The reason Coach Royal wanted me to be the recruiting coordinator was because Barry Switzer at Oklahoma had put Jerry Pettibone in that position and he was having success bringing kids to Norman," recalled Dabbs. "Coach Royal wanted to make sure that we had that same advantage. I said yes, and I guess you could say the rest is history."

"It was amazing how Coach Dabbs knew every coach in the State of Texas," said Lowry. "Everyone loved him and they still do."

When Earl Campbell won the Heisman Trophy in 1977 and Brad Shearer won the Outland Trophy the same year, Dabbs became the first coach in America to recruit two players that captured those prestigious awards in the same season.

"Coach Dabbs is special," said Campbell. "He's my friend and quite honestly the University of Texas needs to name something in honor of him…he's that special."

TODD DODGE—THOMAS JEFFERSON HIGH SCHOOL—PORT ARTHUR, TEXAS

Todd Dodge has had an outstanding career in Texas high school football as both a player and a coach. Many remember Dodge as a trendsetter, who became the first player in the football-rich state to top 3,000 yards passing in a season.

Todd Russell Dodge was born on July 21, 1963. Dodge moved around a lot as a kid because of his dad's job. Reverend Don Dodge was a Methodist preacher who moved his family to Port Arthur, Texas, between Todd's seventh and eighth grades.

The move wasn't a long one for young Todd, who was an up-and-coming star youth football quarterback in West Orange, about 30 miles northeast of Port Arthur. However, when Dodge went out for the eighth-grade team, he found himself on the B-Team and a backup quarterback at that.

"I was a kid that absolutely drank in the game of football," said Dodge. "I loved to throw the football."

Eventually, Dodge worked his way to becoming the starter of the A-Team in eighth grade, but when he entered high school he once again found himself on the B-Team. Dodge said his circumstances changed when Ronnie Thompson took over the Port Arthur program as head coach of Thomas Jefferson High School between Todd's freshman and sophomore seasons.

Thompson was a Port Arthur native. He played on the same Thomas Jefferson team as College Football Hall of Fame coach Jimmy Johnson, who led the Dallas Cowboys to two Super Bowl victories, plus a national championship while at the University of Miami [FL]. Back then, Port Arthur High was led by head coach Clarence "Buckshot" Underwood, who came to Port Arthur after coaching at the University of Kentucky.

"Ronnie was a visionary," said Dodge. "He said he had an idea that he wanted to start throwing the football before throwing it was cool. Coach Thompson started me out on the JV team my sophomore year, and halfway through that season, he moved me up. We called it the big youth movement, because he moved about nine sophomores into starting positions."

While the changes didn't make a big difference in wins and losses, Dodge said the team won its final game to finish 1–9.

"He threw us young pups to the wolves," said Dodge. "However, we started chunking the ball around and we knew we had all these sophomores coming back next season, plus a pretty good junior class that would be seniors the next year."

Dodge's teammate and favorite receiver was Brent Duhon, who followed him to the University of Texas after graduating. Like Dodge, Duhon was one of the first sophomores moved into the starting lineup in 1978.

"I think I was the first sophomore to be moved into the starting lineup," remembered Duhon. "It was the third game of my sophomore season. As a thrower, I guess the first time I really saw how well Todd threw the football was going into our sophomore year. In the summer the two of us would be throwing four or five times a week. We'd stay after practice and work out just so we could get on the same page. Our coaches did a great job during practice where we'd catch a ton of balls every day. Back then, if you were a wide receiver, you'd catch about ten balls per practice, but for us, I'd say we were catching seventy or eighty balls a practice."

The youth movement worked for Thompson as Jefferson went 6–4 during Dodge's junior season, which brought back pride to the program that had fallen on hard times for quite a few years. Dodge passed for over 2,000 yards as a junior.

"Port Arthur really was one of those historically great Texas high school football areas that had really fallen by the wayside, and Coach Thompson and my teammates were able to restore that pride, which is something I'm very proud of," said Dodge. "We were throwing the ball twenty to thirty times a game when everyone else was running the wishbone or veer.

"The one thing that I appreciated about my Coach [Thompson] and I still keep it as a philosophy today is to spread the wealth offensively. We spread the ball around to a lot of different players. Brent [Duhon], of course, caught a lot of balls and set lots of records with me, but we always got everyone into the offense."

As a senior quarterback at Thomas Jefferson High, Dodge led his team to the 1980 Class 5A state championship game against Odessa Permian High School. Yes, the same team that about a decade later would be spotlighted in Buzz Bissinger's book *Friday Night Lights: A Town, a Team, and a Dream.*

"Todd's quality was always his leadership," recalled Duhon, who caught a state-record 89 passes during his senior season. "He wasn't a big yeller or screamer, but everyone followed him. Everyone respected him, and that was a special season."

"Todd could run, and he threw the ball so accurately," recalled University of Texas recruiting coordinator Kenneth Dabbs, who recruited Dodge and Duhon along with two other Jefferson players off the 1980 team. "He threw the perfect football, in my opinion. But I'll tell you what, Brent Duhon was as good a short receiver as you'll ever find. He caught everything Todd threw."

Dodge said that 1980 season was special, not only because of playing for a state title but because the team had gone from 1–9 two years prior to 14–0 and No. 1 in the state heading into the Permian game. The state championship appearance was the first in twenty-three years for Thomas Jefferson. Permian had won two state championships in the past fifteen years.

Coming into the state championship contest, Dodge had already broken almost every high school state record for passing yards in a single season. In the first 14 games, Dodge threw for 2,935 yards.

"My coach was up on the history of all of it [state records]," recalled Dodge. "He would keep us up on it, but not in a bad way. It was more of a motivating way. I was just a country kid from Port Arthur and we didn't get out much, but at the time, I knew exactly who Gary Kubiak [St. Pius X] and Tommy Kraemer [San Antonio Robert E. Lee High School] were. However, the records weren't a big deal. I do recall that during my recruiting visit to Texas A&M, Gary [Kubiak] was my host, and I remember being star struck.

"Quite honestly, my biggest game memory from that run to the state championship came in the opening round at the Astrodome against Aldine High School," added Dodge. "We won 49–7, but I remember I threw for 330-some yards and we started the game completing 23-of-23 passes. They [Aldine] were 10–0 coming into the game, and that win was a tremendous boost for our team for the rest of the playoffs."

The championship game itself is bittersweet for Dodge, who left Texas Stadium on the losing side of a 28–19 decision. Jefferson led 19–7 at the half against a Panthers' defense that had only given up 4.3 points a game with nine shutouts. Permian dominated the second half, but Dodge did become the first player in Texas high school football history to surpass 3,000 yards passing in a season.

Dodge finished the 1980 season with 3,131 yards, completing 221-of-358 passes with 30 touchdowns. His 5,693 career passing yards broke Kramer's old public-school record. Kubiak was a four-year starter at St. Pius X, a private school, and held the overall record with 6,190 yards passing.

Dodge and Duhon, who finished his career with 180 catches, appeared in *Sports Illustrated*'s "Faces in the Crowd" in late January 1981.

"Todd had all of the speed and brains to play at the NFL level and run a professional offense," said Duhon, who had an NFL tryout with the Chicago Bears. "Back then, NFL teams didn't look at someone like Todd because of his height, which was probably just under 6-feet tall. But he had all of the qualities and leadership to play at the next level, and I have no doubt in my mind that he could have played in the NFL, but he wasn't 6-foot-3 or 6-foot-4."

Dodge's love of the high school game is evidenced by the fact that shortly after graduating from Texas, he went into high school coaching at Rockwall High School at twenty-two years of age. As the team's quarterback and wide receivers coach, he helped Rockwall reach the 4A state championship game in 1987. In the early '90s, as the offensive coordinator at McKinney High School, he developed a hybrid offense that was a cross between the University of Houston's Run-and-Shoot offense and the University of Miami's (Florida) three-to-five stop drop with a zone running game. Dodge is known as a coach that has mastered the spread offense.

As a head coach, Dodge led Southlake Carroll High School to four state championships and two "mythical" national championships. With the Dragons, he continued his legacy as a coach who knew how to operate a wide-open, high-powered offense which threw the ball all over the field. Dodge left Carroll to become the head coach at the University of North Texas in 2007 but returned to the high school game in 2012. He's currently the head coach at Westlake High School in Austin, which is Drew Brees's alma mater.

"One of my great memories of my coaching career, to this point, is that I've been able to coach nine different quarterbacks who have been the Offensive Player of the Year in the state of Texas," said Dodge. "The other thing that needs to be mentioned, though, is how much Coach Thompson did for me—not only as a player, but also making me want to coach. A lot of people may not know his name, but there's no doubt in my mind that he needs to be recognized as one of the true innovators in our state when it comes to the passing game."

After High School

Todd Dodge attended the University of Texas, playing quarterback under head coach Fred Akers. He began his career as a backup quarterback as a freshman, although he did start the 1982 Sun Bowl against North Carolina when starter Robert Brewer broke his hand five days before the game in El Paso, Texas.

Dodge won the starting job as a sophomore, but a shoulder injury in Texas' final preseason scrimmage sidelined him for the team's opener. He finally reclaimed the starting role from Rob Moershell for a couple of games in November but was moved to the backup role later in the month on a team that finished undefeated, losing to Georgia in the Cotton Bowl.

In his junior year, Texas rose to No. 1 in the national rankings with Dodge as the starter. However, after a 6–0–1 start, he hit a rough patch and found himself back in the backup role.

JOHNATHAN GRAY—ALEDO HIGH SCHOOL— ALEDO, TEXAS

Jonathan Gray was a touchdown machine who gained yardage in large chunks every time he touched the ball. The Aledo High School running back is America's all-time leader in touchdowns and second in points scored. Gray, with 205 touchdowns, is also fifth on the all-time career rushing list with 10,889 yards from

2008 to 2011. He's second all-time in the state of Texas, behind Ken Hall (who you'll hear about later on in this chapter).

While Gray, who went on to play at the University of Texas, has many memorable moments, it's hard to top the 2010 Texas Class 4A Division II championship game. I was at this game when the junior sliced-and-diced the La Marque High School defense for 325 rushing yards with eight touchdowns in a 69–34 win before 27,330 fans at Cowboys Stadium.

"I remember that before the game, we all sat down and prayed," recalled Gray. "We were talking about going for our second-straight state title and how hard we'd have to work to get a win. It's still hard to believe my numbers that game, but what I will tell you is that my offensive line was outstanding that night."

What made the performance even better was the fact that Gray was struggling with an injured knee and hadn't run the ball in practice for the three weeks leading up to the game.

"He was outstanding that night," recalled former *Houston Chronicle* sportswriter Sam Kahn, who covered that championship game. "He was unstoppable."

Not only did Gray and his teammates win their second-straight title, but they also got the three-peat in 2011 when the Bearcats beat Manvel 49–28. He closed out his career as the state's all-time leader in single-season and career touchdowns.

Incredibly, Gray topped the 100-yard rushing mark 51 times, which is a state record. He also holds the record for career carries with 1,225.

As far as the long list of records, Gray said it's not a big deal. "A record is fun to have, but it's not something I think about all the time. Maybe when I'm older, they'll mean something. I'm just proud of what we accomplished as a team."

Gray was also the first junior to win ESPN's Mr. Football USA Award in 2010. He also became the first two-time winner after the 2011 season.

When I asked Gray how he likes to be remembered by coaches, teammates, and Texas high school football fans he said, "I want them to say that I was a nice person, a great athlete, and a humble person."

After High School

Johnathan Gray attended the University of Texas after graduating from Aledo. A five-star recruit in high school, Gray appeared destined for the NFL, but two tears of his Achilles tendon all but ended his professional football aspirations. During his career as a Longhorn, he rushed for 2,607 yards with 17 touchdowns. Gray has already been inducted into the Texas High School Football Hall of Fame.

KENNETH HALL—SUGAR LAND HIGH SCHOOL— SUGAR LAND, TEXAS

It's been more than six decades since Ken Hall of Sugar Land High School stepped on a high school football field, but his name is well-known as the Lone Star State's all-time leading rusher with 11,232 yards from 1950 to 1953. Hall's career yardage mark also placed him at the top of America's all-time list until current Tennessee Titans running back Derrick Henry broke the record in 2012 while playing at Yulee High School near Jacksonville, Florida.

Charles Kenneth Hall, who was nicknamed the "Sugar Land Express," was born on December 13, 1935. He set seventeen national records during his high school football career.

Like so many of the players we've talked with for this book, football wasn't first and foremost on Hall's mind. He said that he started playing football in the eighth grade.

"I'm not even sure why I went out," said Hall. "I didn't care anything about it [football]. I didn't know anything about it. I didn't know the rules. Heck, I didn't even know that you couldn't throw a ball to a lineman."

"I was slow," Hall added. "The concept of football just didn't appeal to me. I would much rather march in the band and play the trumpet. And that's basically what I did starting in the sixth grade through high school."

Playing in the band is where Hall met his wife Gloria, who he calls "Honey." The two celebrated their sixty-second anniversary in December 2017. He said one of his best memories isn't from the football field but during his sophomore season when he was elected captain for one of the games and she was voted the "football sweetheart" that same night. Hall laughed recalling the fact that at halftime of that game, he was able to give her a kiss on the cheek during the ceremony.

Hall recalled that the only reason he even tried out for football was because B. I. Webb, who was a senior, told him they were going to work out together to get ready for the upcoming football season that began in a couple of weeks. Hall said he wasn't the least bit interested, but Webb insisted.

"First thing we did was run about fifteen laps around the goal-posts," said Hall. "By the end, I couldn't breathe and told him, 'No, I don't want to do this.' Well, it's a long story, but let's just say that I was convinced to play."

Hall said the one thing that he could do, even though he claims at that time that he couldn't walk a straight line and chew gum at the same time, was throw and kick the football. He said he didn't care one bit about running with the ball.

"I saw people getting hurt running the ball, and I didn't want that to happen to me," said Hall. "So, because I could throw, they put me at quarterback. However, it didn't work well. Instead, the coach, Dugan Hightower, decided to start a senior at quarterback for the start of the season."

Hall recalled that the team lost its first five games. He said Coach Hightower put him in for the next game and said, "Do what you can." By that time, Hall said he had gotten a little faster, but he was still more interested in throwing the ball than running it.

"I remember early in the game, I dropped back to pass," said Hall. "I looked around, and nobody was open, so I decided to run the ball."

That play resulted in Hall scoring on a 76-yard run—and he never stopped running.

"After scoring, I turned around and looked at the guys that had been chasing me and they were back pretty far," said Hall. "I remember thinking to myself that that was fun...maybe we should do this again sometime. I scored another touchdown before the game was over and that's how it all started."

It also helped that Hall had a growth spurt between eighth grade and his freshman year. As an eighth-grader, Hall was 5-foot-6 and weighed only 135 pounds. Heading into his freshman year, he had shot up six inches to an even 6-foot and weighed 186 pounds.

That growth spurt was also accompanied by a burst of speed. Hall said in the 100-yard dash in the eighth grade, his best time was 12.5 seconds. As a freshman, he was clocked at 10.1 seconds. He said that running in track was something he enjoyed more than football.

The last four games of his freshman season, after taking over as the team's starting quarterback, Hall's credited with rushing for over 500 yards and scoring 72 points. Sugar Land finished a perfect 4–0 with Hall at the offensive controls, outscoring their opponents 131–7.

Jerry Cooper was Hall's teammate at Sugar Land. He was two years behind Ken in high school, and the two are good friends to this day.

"Kenneth could run like a rabbit," recalled Cooper, who played wingback. "He was just a natural. He never picked up a weight, but that's because we didn't have any in the gym. He had big hands, and the thing I recall is he was such a nice guy. I remember times when he'd run over a defensive player tackling him, and then Kenneth would help him up. That got the coaches a little angry, but that was just the way he was and still is…a nice guy."

Going into Hall's sophomore year, the coaches changed the offense from the T-formation to the Notre Dame Box, which is a variation of the Single-Wing formation. It had two tight ends and four backs, and usually featured an unbalanced line. The players would line up in the T-formation and then shift into the box.

Hall was shifted to the tailback position in Sugar Land's new offense. He said they didn't have a big squad as far as numbers, but he said they had a lot of quality athletes. During that season, Hall's teammate, who was the blocking back in the formation, called the offensive plays and then Ken took over those duties as a junior and senior.

"We didn't get plays in from the sideline," said Hall. "We'd practice all week so that when it came game time, we knew what we were doing out there.

"The one thing that gave us an advantage is that we really were the only team in the area that ran the Single-Wing, so our opponents' defense only had a week to prepare to play against it," Hall added.

When Hall did become the team's play caller, he said he wasn't selfish or interested in padding his stats. He said by the end of the game, everyone had carried the ball about the same amount. Hall, who is a member of the Texas High School Football Hall of Fame and the Texas Sports Hall of Fame, also estimated that he probably threw the ball about four or five times a game, which added up to over 3,000 yards passing during his career.

His nickname of the "Sugar Land Express" reportedly evolved from a sportswriter who had written that Hall ran like a freight train. Hall said it kind of grew from there.

The most amazing thing about Hall's numbers is they could have been much greater had it not been for the fact that Sugar Land was blowing out most of its opponents, leaving Hall and the first-teamers on the bench in the second half.

"On the average, I played about a half of a game," recalled Hall. "The great thing was our backups were pretty darn good, too, and had their own fun running the ball. I really don't recall how many carries I had in my career, but if I carried the ball more than twenty times in a game, that would be a lot. My teammates knew how to knock them down, and I knew how to run by them."

One of the most talked-about games during Ken's career was against Houston Lutheran when Hall scored a national single-game record of 49 points by scoring seven touchdowns and kicking seven extra points. In about only one half of action, Hall ran for 520 yards, averaging 47.3 yards per carry with only eleven carries. He scored on a kickoff and punt return, plus he returned an interception for a score and had 687 yards in total offense.

"That was a quite a game," said Cooper. "There's no telling how many touchdowns he would have scored if he played more than the first half."

Cooper said that football in those days in the community was fun, with everyone enjoying the exploits of the team. During Hall's career, Sugar Land would win three straight Class B regional championships. Back in the early '50s, a regional championship was all a small school like Sugar Land could play for. From the 1950 season through Hall's final year in 1953, Sugar Land was 37–6–1. If you remove the five losses before Hall took over at quarterback, Sugar Land was 37–1–1. That one loss occurred when Hall missed a game due to a neck injury.

"The Lions Club would always feed us for our away games," said Cooper. "We'd eat chicken fried steak before we left. By the time we got back from the game, the dining room would be packed with people and we'd eat some more chicken fried steak."

Statistically, Hall's senior season running the football still ranks as one of the best all-time in Texas and the nation. His 4,045 yards on the ground is still Texas' all-time single season record and ranks sixth nationally. His 47.3 yard average per carry in the Houston Lutheran game is still the highest recorded in high school football, while his 337.1 yards rushing per game is third all-time nationally. He averaged 32.9 points per game during the 1953 season, which is still a national record. His 4.8 touchdowns per game are fifth all-time in America.

"The most amazing thing about that year," recalled Cooper. "The other guys on the team combined for 4,000 more yards rushing. 8,000 yards rushing in a season is pretty impressive.

"Kenneth could do anything he wanted on the field," Cooper added. "I remember one game when our opponent called a time-out. Their coach was a little ruffled and asked his player, 'Who called the time-out?' The player evidently replied that he did because he was dead beat from running up and down the field trying to catch Kenneth. If Kenneth played the whole game, we would have scored 100 points quite a few times."

That 1953 season was made even more amazing by the fact that Sugar Land only had seventeen players on its roster.

When Hall left Sugar Land's gridiron, he had accounted for 14,558 yards in total offense, with 11,232 rushing yards and 3,326 passing yards. That total offense yardage stood as a national record until 1998, when future Major League Baseball catcher J. R. House broke it when he played at Nitro High School in West Virginia.

Hall amassed thirty-eight 100-yard rushing games during his career, which stood as a national record until the mid-'80s when future Pro Football Hall of Famer Emmitt Smith topped the mark when he was playing at Escambia High School in Florida.

When Derrick Henry, who went on to win the Heisman Trophy at the University of Alabama, was stalking Hall for the record in 2012, Hall's early '50s accomplishments were brought back into the spotlight with numerous major media outlets like ESPN calling him for comments on Henry and asking him to recall his exploits on the field.

Hall said the most asked question he gets is "What was it like?"

"We were just a bunch of kids," said Hall. "We were good athletes that liked each other. We really loved one another. Our coaches were fantastic at making sure we understood that athletics can do a whole lot more for you than just win games."

After High School

Hall chose to attend Texas A&M after high school, where the legendary Paul "Bear" Bryant was the school's head football coach. Hall quit the team to get married to Gloria before Bryant took the team to its summer football camp in 1954 in Junction, Texas. A book called *The Junction Boys* was written about that camp. The Junction Boys is the name given to the players that made it through the entire camp. It is reported that of over the one hundred or so players that went to Junction, only twenty-seven to thirty-eight actually stayed with the team.

Between 1957 and 1961, Hall played in the Canadian Football League and for the Chicago Cardinals (NFL), Houston Oilers (AFL), and then the St. Louis Cardinals (NFL). He rushed for only 212 yards during his NFL career, averaging 1.5 yards per carry and scoring one touchdown. He was a solid kickoff returner, averaging 26.9 yards per return over his career with one touchdown. Hall also served as Houston's punter averaging 32 yards per punt in 1960 and 1961.

ALAN LOWRY—IRVING HIGH SCHOOL—
IRVING, TEXAS

Like Bill Bradley featured earlier, Alan Lowry was one of the top Texas high school football players. Like Bradley, Lowry, who played for the legendary Ken Dabbs when he was the head coach at Irving High School, excelled at multiple sports.

"One of my memories from high school was during my senior year when we lost in the state quarterfinals and then the next day I started basketball practice. Then the next Tuesday, a couple days later, I played in a basketball game," chuckled Lowry, who also was a very good baseball player.

Alan D. Lowry was born on November 21, 1950, in Miami, Oklahoma. He began playing football in seventh grade as a running back but the next year he moved to quarterback. Lowry said he enjoyed playing more than just quarterback.

"For Coach Dabbs, I was the quarterback, the safety, the kick returner, the kicker, and the punter," said Lowry, who would leave Irving High School with a scholarship to the University of Texas.

Dabbs took over the reins of the Irving High program for the 1968 season after serving as an assistant coach the previous year under head coach Tom Gray. Lowry said that the team underperformed during the 1967 season, going 6–4 in a run-first, throw-second Wing-T offense. Lowry only threw the ball 77 times in

1967, and the Tigers did not make the playoffs. He said that Dabbs made an immediate impact when he took over the team.

"He really was fun to play for because he was such a players' coach," said Lowry. "He did everything he could to use every one of the players the best that he could. He basically changed our entire offense to fit me. He put in the Houston Veer that Bill Yeoman was running at Houston, and it worked very well for us. You could say it was the perfect move."

"Alan was as good an option quarterback in the United States as there was at that time," said Dabbs. "He never came off the field. He played free safety on defense. He did the punting and the kickoffs. He was A to A+ in everything he did."

With Lowry usually topping the century mark in rushing, Irving put together a 9–1 regular season. The Tigers' only blemish was a 26–21 non-district loss to Garland. Irving opened the Class 4A playoffs with a 35–28 win over Wichita Falls, and then the Tigers beat Richardson, which was ranked No. 5 in the state, 14–12.

"Against Wichita Falls the game was tied (28–28), and they let us score because we led on penetrations," said Lowry. "The next game against Richardson, we won with just twelve seconds to go and I think the Odessa Permian coaches had already left the stadium taking all the Richardson stuff with them because they thought we were going to lose."

Lowry recalled the state quarterfinal game against Permian as a great memory because the team actually flew from the Fort Worth area to West Texas.

"It was something [fly] that none of us had done before," Lowry said. "There were a lot of people that had never been on an airplane, and I remember walking into that high school stadium with 20,000 seats was pretty amazing. Actually, the whole trip was amazing."

Unfortunately, Irving's magical run came to an end in West Texas that day. The Panthers used a ball control offense that only threw three passes, with none of them coming in the second half before 15,000 fans. Permian took a 10–0 lead into the fourth quarter, which is when Irving scored off a Panther turnover to cut the lead to 10–6, but that was the last score in the game.

"That was an amazing time in my life," said Lowry. "It's one of the best times that I can remember, especially with my family being a part of it. It really was an amazing time."

After High School

Lowry was highly recruited during his senior season. He chose Texas over Oklahoma and Texas Christian University, where he played football and baseball.

During his sophomore and junior years, Lowry played defensive back and then switched to quarterback for his senior season in 1972. He led the Longhorns to a 10–1 record and a No. 3 overall ranking. The team's only loss came against No. 2 Oklahoma in their school's legendary Red River Rivalry.

Lowry was drafted in the 13th round of the 1973 NFL Draft by the New England Patriots as a quarterback but never played again because of nerve damage in his right arm. That injury started him on a long coaching career that began at Texas. At the professional level, Lowery won a Super Bowl ring with the 49ers as the team's special teams coach in Super Bowl XXIX. He's also known as the mastermind of the "Music City Miracle" in the

2000 NFL playoff game between Lowry's Tennessee Titans and the Buffalo Bills.

22

Prairie View Interscholastic League

AS MENTIONED IN several sections of this book, the Prairie View Interscholastic League (PVIL) played the leading role in developing African American student-athletes like "Mean Joe" Greene, Ken Houston, and Elmo Wright.

The PVIL began in 1920 as the Texas Interscholastic League of Colored Schools. The PVIL held state championship games in baseball, basketball, football, and track. In 1965, the University Interscholastic League (UIL), which governed only the white schools, admitted PVIL schools along with allowing them to compete with UIL schools starting with the 1967-68 school year. The UIL fully absorbed all the PVIL schools for the 1971-72 school year.

At its peak, the PVIL reportedly covered 500 schools. A newspaper report at the start of the 1958 season indicated that there were 137 schools in the PVIL with over 6,000 student-athletes.

In addition to Greene, Houston, and Wright, the PVIL produced stars like Cliff Branch, Mel Farr, Abner Haynes, Jerry LeVias, Bubba Smith, Charlie Taylor, Otis Taylor, Emmitt Thomas, Gene Upshaw (who was a better baseball player who played only one year of high school football at Robstown High School), and Gene Washington. Joining Greene and Houston in the Pro Football Hall of Fame there are four other PVIL stars: Dick "Night Train" Lane, Charlie Taylor, Thomas, and Upshaw.

Ironically, after the integration of the Prairie View Interscholastic League and the UIL, four former PVIL players were taken in the first round of the NFL Draft. Bubba Smith was selected No. 1 overall by the Baltimore Colts, followed by Mel Farr, who was drafted No. 7 by the Detroit Lions. The Minnesota Vikings drafted Gene Washington with the No. 8 pick. The Oakland Raiders chose Gene Upshaw with the 17th overall pick.

In 1992, the *Houston Chronicle* selected an all-time PVIL team:

Offense:

WR: Charley Taylor, Grand Prairie Dalworth HS
WR: Warren Wells, Beaumont Hebert HS
WR: Cliff Branch, Houston Worthing HS
End: Jerry LeVias, Beaumont Hebert HS
Line: Gene Upshaw, Robstown HS

Line: Marvin Upshaw, Robstown HS
Line: Ernie Ladd, Orange HS
Line: Clarence Williams, Sweeny Carver HS
QB: Otis Taylor, Houston, Worthing HS
Back: Gene Washington, Baytown Carver HS
Back: Duane Thomas, Dallas Lincoln HS

Defense:

Line: Toby Smith, Beaumont Charlton-Pollard HS
Line: Bubba Smith, Beaumont Charlton-Pollard HS
Line: Joe Greene, Temple Dunbar HS
Line: Harvey Martin, Dallas South Oak Cliff HS
LB: Dick Lane, Austin Anderson HS
LB: Tony Gillory, Beaumont Hebert HS
LB: Emmitt Thomas, Angleton HS
Back: Mel Farr, Beaumont Hebert HS
Back: Miller Farr, Beaumont Hebert HS
Back: Ken Houston, Lufkin Dunbar HS
Back: Abner Haynes, Dallas Lincoln HS

Unfortunately, as many of these players and their teams were not reported on by newspapers back then, I thought it was important to highlight some of the accomplishments by the PIVL's top players.

CLIFF BRANCH—WORTHING HIGH SCHOOL— HOUSTON, TEXAS

It's hard to say whether Cliff Branch was a sprinter who could catch a football or a wide receiver who could sprint. Either way,

Branch was one of the fastest high school football players to take to the gridiron in the Lone Star State.

Clifford Branch was born on August 1, 1948, in Houston, Texas. He played high school football at Worthing High School. Branch's coach in both football and track was Oliver Brown, who passed away in 2013.

Branch's track career in high school seemed to transcend his time on the gridiron. He was the PVIL's 100-yard dash title in 1966 and 1967 and is credited with being the first Texas high school runner to break the 10-second barrier with a sprint of 9.3 seconds.

After High School

After a year of junior college football, Branch landed a scholarship from the University of Colorado. In Boulder, Branch set an NCAA record with eight kickoff returns. He also set a record in the 100-meter dash at the 1972 NCAA championships with a time of 10 seconds flat.

The Oakland Raiders selected Branch with the 98th overall pick in the fourth round of the 1972 NFL Draft. He played his entire career with the Oakland/Los Angeles Raiders and is the only player to have been a member on all three Raider Super Bowl champion teams.

JERRY LEVIAS—HEBERT HIGH SCHOOL—BEAUMONT, TEXAS

Like Cliff Branch, Jerry LeVias could flat-out run. LeVias was born on September 5, 1946, in Beaumont, Texas, where he attended the all-black Hebert High School.

At less than 120 pounds in junior high, LeVias, who would become the first African American scholarship athlete in the Southwest Conference in 1965, needed to convince his coaches that he could play the game. Because of his size, LeVias didn't start playing football until he was in the eighth grade.

By the time he graduated from Hebert High, LeVias was a robust 5-foot-8, 148 pounds. He was named to the First Team Black All-State squad as a junior and a senior.

The cherry on the sundae in high school came when LeVias was chosen to play for an integrated Texas All-Star team that played a team of Pennsylvania All-Stars in a showcase called the Big 33 Classic in Hershey, Pennsylvania. The Big 33 Classic began in 1958 and, since that time, Pennsylvania's best football players have been playing all-star teams from Maryland, Ohio, and Texas. On occasion, the Keystone State has taken on an all-USA team. Up and through Super Bowl LII between the New England Patriots and the Philadelphia Eagles, there's never been a Super Bowl played without Big 33 alum, which makes it the quintessential high school football all-star game.

The '65 game was the second in the series between the two football powerhouse states, with Pennsylvania winning 12–6 in 1964. That outcome didn't sit too well with the powers that be in Texas high school football, who wanted to make sure that they could claim the bragging rights to which state played the best high school football.

How serious were the Texans? First, they changed the date of the sacred Texas High School Coaches Association's North-South All-Star game so that all the top players could participate in the Big 33. Second, Texas employed former NFL and Texas high school stars Bobby Layne and Doak Walker to coach the all-stars.

"Bobby was fit to be tied because he had lost the Big 33 game the year before," said Bill Bradley of Palestine High who, despite his quarterback skills, was picked to play safety and punt for the Big 33 team.

Bradley and LeVias made history that week in Hershey when "Super Bill" agreed to room with LeVias. While such a statement doesn't seem like a big deal today, back in 1965, Texas was still a segregated state.

"We're still friends to this day," said Bradley. "We bonded during the Big 33 week, and nothing has changed."

As far as the game, Bradley was quickly inserted at quarterback after Texas fell behind 3–0 in the first quarter. After that, the two roommates began connecting on the field. The first touchdown pass between the two gave Texas the lead at 7–3. That score marked the first time that Pennsylvania had surrendered a point against an out-of-state team in the history of the Big 33 game that started with Pennsylvania shutting out an all-USA All-Star team in 1958 and 1959.

After High School

LeVias attended SMU on a scholarship, which was the first given by a Southwest Conference team to an African American player. He played for the Houston Oilers during the 1969 and 1970 seasons. From 1971 through the 1974 season, LeVias played with the San Diego Chargers. He was elected to the Texas Sports Hall of Fame in 1995, the College Football Hall of Fame in 2003, and the Texas High School Football Hall of Fame in 2014.

BUBBA SMITH—CHARLTON-POLLARD HIGH SCHOOL—BEAUMONT, TEXAS

Charles Aaron "Bubba" Smith was born on February 28, 1945, and played at Charlton-Pollard High School in Beaumont, Texas, in the early '60s. Charlton-Pollard was one of two black high schools in Beaumont. Hebert High School was the other, and the two schools met in the Soul Bowl in the '60s and '70s. The game became so big that at one point it was moved to Lamar University's Cardinal Stadium that seated 19,000 to accommodate the large crowds.

Smith, who was the NFL's No. 1 overall draft pick in 1967 by the Baltimore Colts, entered high school as a normal-size kid. He was 5-feet-9 but shot up to 6-feet-7 by the time he left high school.

Bubba Smith played for his father, Willie Ray Smith Sr., who was a great high school coach, amassing 235 victories at three schools. The elder Smith, who never played the game himself, was said to be a tough, old-school coach who wasn't afraid to take off his leather belt to slap players on the butt when they were making mistakes on the field.

Between Bubba, his dad, and Bubba's two brothers, Ray Jr. and Toby, who also played in the NFL, Charlton-Pollard became a Texas high school football powerhouse. Bubba began playing football in the seventh grade.

As a senior, Bubba and his brothers helped dad finish with a perfect 11–0 record and a No. 1 ranking in the state. Many call Smith one of the best players to ever put on a Texas high school football uniform.

After High School

Because the Southwest Conference wasn't offering scholarships to black athletes, Smith accepted a scholarship to Michigan State University. The Baltimore Colts picked Smith No. 1 overall in the 1967 NFL Draft. He played with the Colts, Oakland Raiders, and Houston Oilers during his career from 1967 to 1976. After retirement, Smith became an actor known for his performances in the *Police Academy* movies. He passed away in 2011.

CHARLEY TAYLOR—DALWORTH HIGH SCHOOL— GRAND PRAIRIE, TEXAS

Charles Robert Taylor was born on September 28, 1941, in Grand Prairie, Texas. He was the second of seven children.

Taylor began his sports career in eighth grade playing baseball, basketball, football, and track. He played at Dalworth High School, the segregated high school in Grand Prairie. In 1958, Taylor and the Dalworth Dragons had an outstanding season, advancing to the Prairie Valley Interscholastic League 1A championship game against Livingston Dunbar.

While there aren't a lot of newspaper reports from that year, Taylor was listed as a 187-pound fullback during his senior season in 1958. In a 39–6 win over St. Peter's in September, Taylor scored two touchdowns as the Dragons amassed 464 yards rushing as a team. In mid-October, the *Grand Prairie Daily News* ran a headline, "Taylor, Hale, Big Runs in Dalworth's 28–12 victory." The game story reported that Taylor scored a touchdown, a two-point conversion, and intercepted five Garland High passes.

Taylor and his Dalworth teammates entered the 1958 championship game with a 10–1–1 record while Dunbar, located near Houston, was undefeated. Dalworth's defense was strong, giving up only a touchdown per game in the first eleven games of the season. Taylor scored a couple of rushing touchdowns in the game, but it wasn't enough as Dunbar captured the championship with a 26–24 victory.

Taylor was honored for an outstanding season by being named to the first team All-District 3-AAA football team.

After High School

Arizona State University offered Taylor a scholarship after high school. He played running back and defensive back for the Sun Devils. Taylor was named an All-American as a junior and senior.

The Washington Redskins selected Taylor with the third overall pick in the 1964 NFL Draft. He was named the United Press International Rookie of the Year. The Redskins switched Taylor from running back to wide receiver in 1966. When he retired, he was the NFL's all-time leader in receptions with 649 and was elected to the Pro Football Hall of Fame in 1984.

24

The Top Texas High School Football Teams Sending Players to the NFL

I BEGAN WITH A lot of statistics and I'll close with a look at which Texas high schools have placed the most players in the NFL, according to the latest numbers from Pro-Football-Reference.com.

Ball High School in Galveston and South Oak Cliff in Dallas lead the Lone Star State with twenty-four current and former NFL players. Ball and SOC are currently tied with three other teams across America for eleventh on the all-time list that is led by Long Beach Poly of California, which has 56 current and for-mer NFL players.

As of the 2017 season, only Ball High School had a player on an active roster. That's Tampa Bay wide receiver Mike Evans, who was the No. 7 overall pick in first round of the 2014 NFL Draft.

Like so many aforementioned athletes, Evans began playing football late. He only played his senior season for the Ball Tor-nadoes. His 25 receptions for 648 yards and seven touchdowns were good enough to catch the eye of Texas A&M, which offered him a scholarship. Evans also played basketball and ran track at Ball, as well as participated in jumping events in track and field.

Aside from Evans, below are the twenty-three other Tornadoes that have played in the NFL:

BALL HIGH SCHOOL TORNADOES NFL ALUMNI

Player, Position—Teams (Years)
Mike Evans, WR—Tampa Bay (2014–present)
Casey Hampton, NT-DT—Pittsburgh (2001–2012)
Derrick Pope, LB—Miami (2004–2007)
George McCullough, DB—Tennessee, San Francisco (1997–2001)
Kimble Anders, RB—Kansas City (1991–2000)
Tim Denton, DB—Washington, San Diego (1998–2000)
Rodney Artmore, DB—Green Bay (1999)
Eric Hill, LB—Phoenix, Arizona, St. Louis Rams, San Diego (1989–1999)

Patrise Alexander, LB—Washington (1996–1998)

Terry Irving, LB—Arizona (1994–1998)

Anthony Phillips, DB—Atlanta, Minnesota (1994–1998)

Todd Scott, DB—Minnesota, Tampa Bay, Kansas City, New York Jets (1991–1997)

Patrick Bates, DB—Los Angeles Raiders, Atlanta (1993–1996)

Robert Williams, DB—Dallas, Kansas City (1987–1993)

Carl Hilton, TE—Minnesota (1986–1989)

Vince Courville, WR—Dallas (1987)

Whitney Paul, LB-DE—Kansas City, New Orleans (1976–1986)

Charles Alexander, RB—Cincinnati (1979–1985)

Thomas Brown, DE-NT—Philadelphia, Cleveland (1980–1983)

Mike Holmes, DB-WR—San Francisco, Buffalo, Miami (1974–1976)

Harold Paul, T—San Diego (1974)

Ken Pope, DB—New England (1974)

Billy Stevens, QB—Green Bay (1968–1969)

Joe Magliolo, LB—New York Yankees (1948)

The last full-time player in the NFL for South Oak Cliff High School was Rod Jones, who played eleven years in the NFL with Tampa Bay and Cincinnati from 1986 through 1996.

SOUTH OAK CLIFF HIGH SCHOOL GOLDEN BEARS NFL ALUMNI

Player, Position: Teams (Years)
Lendy Holmes, DB: Washington (2009)

LaTarence Dunbar, WR: Atlanta (2003)

Rod Jones, DB: Tampa Bay, Cincinnati (1986–1996)

Joe King, DB: Tampa Bay, Oakland, Cincinnati, Cleveland (1991–1995)

Michael Downs, DB: Dallas, Phoenix (1981–1989)

Ira Albright, NT, RB: Buffalo (1987)

Egypt Allen, DB: Chicago (1987)

Marvin Ayers, DE: Philadelphia (1987)

Cornelius Dozier, DB: Kansas City (1987)

John Preston, DB: St. Louis Cardinals (1987)

Durwood Roquemore, DB: Kansas City, Buffalo (1982–1987)

Gary Spann, LB: Kansas City (1987)

Joe Hayes, RB, WR: Philadelphia (1984)

Wayne Morris, RB: St. Louis Cardinals, San Diego (1976–1984)

Tim Collier, DB: Kansas City, St. Louis Cardinals, San Francisco (1976–1983)

Harvey Martin, DE, DT: Dallas (1973–1983)

Mike Livingston, QB: Kansas City (1968–1979)

Oscar Roan, TE: Cleveland (1975–1978)

Ricky Wesson, DB: Kansas City (1977)

Danny Colbert, DB: San Diego (1974–1976)

Jackie Allen, DB: Oakland, Buffalo, Philadelphia (1969–1972)

Karl Sweetan, QB: Detroit, New Orleans, Los Angeles Rams (1966–1970)

Malcolm Walker, C, T: Dallas, Green Bay (1966–1970)

Guy Reese, DT: Dallas, Baltimore Colts, Atlanta (1962–1966)

What's interesting is that, in spite of all of the NFL players, neither Ball nor South Oak Cliff have ever won a Texas state football championship, which shows how difficult it is to win one.

As of the 2017 NFL season, 839 Texas schools have had at least one player make it to the professional ranks with a total of 2,448 players making it to the NFL.

NFL PLAYERS ALL-TIME BY STATE

State—Schools—Players—Active as of 2017
#1 California—783 schools—2,293 players—241 active players
#2 Texas—839 schools—2,488 players—225 active players
#3 Florida—426 schools—1,594 players—247 active players
#4 Ohio—482 schools—1,489 players—98 active players
#5 Pennsylvania—515 schools—1,403 players—72 active players

Dallas Skyline and Westlake High School in Austin had the most active players during the 2017 season, with each school having four players playing on Sundays. Alief Taylor, Allen, Berkner, DeSoto, Fort Bend Marshall, Klein, North Shore, and Pflugerville had three players each in the league in 2017.

NFL PLAYERS ALL-TIME BY SCHOOLS

School—All Time NFL Players—Active as of 2017
#1 (tied) Ball—24—1
#1 (tied) South Oak Cliff—24—0
#3 (tied) Waco—22—2
#3 (tied) John Tyler—22—2
#5 (tied) Jack Yates—21—0
#5 (tied) Longview—21—2
#7 Temple—19—0
#8 Phillis Wheatley—18—2

#9 (tied) DeSoto—15—3
#9 (tied) Kashmere—15—0
#9 (tied) Dallas Carter—15—1
#9 (tied) Dallas Wilson—15—0
#9 (tied) Lufkin—15—2

DeSoto, led by Von Miller of the Denver Broncos, had three players that played in the NFL in 2017. Todd Peterman, who led DeSoto to its first state championship in 2016, said the one thing that stands out about all the players that have gone to the next level is that they truly were student-athletes.

"Not one of the guys that went on to the next level had grade issues," said Peterman, who resigned from DeSoto at the end of the 2017 season to take the head coach job at Brewer High School in Fort Worth. "We never had to worry about anything off the field, and they were easy to coach.

"The other great thing is that every player has stayed connected to our program. That says a lot and is what makes Texas high school football a beautiful thing."

• • •

Having watched over 1,200 high school football games in person in nineteen different states during my career, I can say that Coach Peterman is absolutely correct about the strong bond that players have to their high school teams and the communities have with their teams and players. In all of my interviews, the players spent more time with me than I had requested. Almost every player said they did longer interviews because they enjoyed reminiscing about things that they hadn't thought of in years.

The Top Texas High School Football Teams Sending Players to the NFL

High school football in Texas is woven into the fabric of every community—no matter how big or how small.

To quote LaDainian Tomlinson: "If you've never been to a Texas high school football game, you may not understand it. From my perspective, when I was playing in high school, I truly felt like I was in the NFL because of the big crowds and the enthusiasm the community had for us. Friday Night Lights really exists. It's almost like the phrase of The Masters [golf tournament]: 'A tradition like no other.'"